Cambridge Elements

Elements in Quantitative Finance
edited by
Riccardo Rebonato
EDHEC Business School

RESAMPLING ASSET PRICES

An Identity-Based Approach

Richard K. Crump
Federal Reserve Bank of New York

Nikolay Gospodinov
Federal Reserve Bank of Atlanta

CAMBRIDGE
UNIVERSITY PRESS

Shaftesbury Road, Cambridge CB2 8EA, United Kingdom

One Liberty Plaza, 20th Floor, New York, NY 10006, USA

477 Williamstown Road, Port Melbourne, VIC 3207, Australia

314–321, 3rd Floor, Plot 3, Splendor Forum, Jasola District Centre, New Delhi – 110025, India

Cambridge University Press is part of Cambridge University Press & Assessment, a department of the University of Cambridge.

We share the University's mission to contribute to society through the pursuit of education, learning and research at the highest international levels of excellence.

www.cambridge.org
Information on this title: www.cambridge.org/9781009738392
DOI: 10.1017/9781009738385

© Richard K. Crump and Nikolay Gospodinov 2026

This publication is in copyright. Subject to statutory exception and to the provisions of relevant collective licensing agreements, no reproduction of any part may take place without the written permission of Cambridge University Press & Assessment.

When citing this work, please include a reference to the DOI 10.1017/9781009738385

First published 2026

A catalogue record for this publication is available from the British Library

A Cataloging-in-Publication data record for this Element is available from the Library of Congress

ISBN 978-1-009-73839-2 Hardback
ISBN 978-1-009-73837-8 Paperback
ISSN 2631-8571 (online)
ISSN 2631-8563 (print)

Cambridge University Press & Assessment has no responsibility for the persistence or accuracy of URLs for external or third-party internet websites referred to in this publication and does not guarantee that any content on such websites is, or will remain, accurate or appropriate.

For EU product safety concerns, contact us at Calle de José Abascal, 56, 1°, 28003 Madrid, Spain, or email eugpsr@cambridge.org

Resampling Asset Prices

An Identity-Based Approach

Elements in Quantitative Finance

DOI: 10.1017/9781009738385
First published online: March 2026

Richard K. Crump
Federal Reserve Bank of New York

Nikolay Gospodinov
Federal Reserve Bank of Atlanta

Author for correspondence: Richard K. Crump, richard.crump@ny.frb.org

Abstract: The authors introduce a novel bootstrap approach to resampling asset price data that can be used for both finite-maturity assets and equities. The key insight is that they bootstrap primitive objects with more appealing statistical properties to avoid resampling series with strong time-series and cross-sectional dependence. They then recover the original dependence structure in an internally consistent manner via definitional identities. Their bootstrap is nonparametric in nature and so avoids the common practice of committing to a tightly parameterized pricing model with explicit assumptions on the form of cross-sectional and time-series dependence. They demonstrate the appealing finite-sample properties of their bootstrap approach in a series of simulation experiments and empirical applications.

Keywords: asset prices, term structure of interest rates, equity markets, resampling-based inference, predictive return regressions

JEL classifications: C15, C58, E43, G10, G12, G17

© Richard K. Crump and Nikolay Gospodinov 2026

ISBNs: 9781009738392 (HB), 9781009738378 (PB), 9781009738385 (OC)
ISSNs: 2631-8571 (online), 2631-8563 (print)

Contents

1 Introduction   1
2 Nominal Yield Curves   8
3 Nominal and Real Yield Curves   27
4 Equities   47
5 Epilogue   76
   List of Notation and Abbreviations   79

   References   80

1 Introduction

Reduced-form econometric models are widely used in asset pricing for predicting future asset returns, estimating risk premia, testing hypotheses implied by economic theory, and so on. However, conducting reliable and valid inference in these models proves challenging. For example, the large-sample asymptotic approximations that are popular in empirical work may suffer from severe distortions when some of the predictors or factors are highly persistent, returns are overlapped over multiple periods, and the model is potentially misspecified. These data characteristics typically manifest themselves in inference that does not fully account for the underlying sources of uncertainty and results in erroneous conclusions such as artificially elevated statistical significance and spurious predictability.

To improve inference, applied researchers now commonly resort to resampling methods that should better mimic and adapt to the salient features of the data in finite samples. However, almost all of the advances in the academic literature have been developed for generic regression models that do not take into account basic definitional relationships linking together the dependent and independent variables in these models. More specifically, predictive regressions of bond returns on lagged yield-based factors, such as the level, slope and curvature of the yield or forward curve, involve variables that are determined jointly and should be resampled in an internally consistent manner respecting definitional identities. Similarly, predictive regressions of equity returns on the dividend yield or dividend-price ratio should impose the identity between returns, dividend growth and the dividend-price ratio in the resampled data.

In this monograph, we capitalize on this observation and propose a novel approach to resampling asset pricing data that is internally consistent and respects the underlying definitional identities that bind the various variables together. It is important to emphasize that this approach is largely nonparametric in nature and does not take a stand on the degree of persistence of the variables, their cross-sectional properties and factor structure, the form of serial correlation and conditional heteroskedasticity in the errors, and so on. All of these data and model characteristics are reestablished by applying the fundamental definitions that relate the variables of interest to the primitive resampled processes. Importantly, these primitive processes are stripped of any strong dependence, and the dependence in the original variables is then recovered entirely from deterministic recursive relationships that involve only the resampled primitive processes and given initial conditions.

1.1 Predictive Return Regressions

The main motivation for this monograph is conducting inference on the regression coefficient(s) in predictive return regressions. In a predictive return regression, future asset returns are assumed to be related to some past set of predictors, that is,

$$\text{RET}_{t,t+h} = \alpha^{(h)} + \beta^{(h)\prime} x_t + e_{t,t+h}, \qquad t = 1, \ldots, T - h. \tag{1.1}$$

Here, $\text{RET}_{t,t+h}$ represents generic asset returns earned over the period from time t to time $t+h$. For fixed-income applications, this is commonly the return earned from holding the asset from time t to time $t + h$, whereas for equity applications this is commonly the sum of the h one-period returns. The predictors, x_t, are generally economic or financial variables that are perceived to have predictive content for future asset returns. We index the regression parameters in equation (1.1) by h as they are commonly estimated for multiple forecast horizons that correspond to different values of h.

The regression in equation (1.1) is typically estimated using ordinary least squares (OLS) and evaluated using the in-sample t-statistic associated with each predictor. The null hypothesis of interest imposes the condition that the ith variable has no predictability, that is, $\beta_i^{(h)} = 0$, with the associated t-statistic

$$t(\beta_i^{(h)}) = \frac{\widehat{\beta}_i^{(h)}}{\text{SE}(\widehat{\beta}_i^{(h)})}, \tag{1.2}$$

where $\text{SE}(\widehat{\beta}_i^{(h)})$ is the standard error of the OLS estimator of $\beta_i^{(h)}$. Assessing whether there is evidence of predictability in asset returns has attracted substantial attention from practitioners and academics alike. In simpler settings, the t-statistic, $t(\beta_i^{(h)})$, should be approximately distributed as a standard normal random variable. However, in predictive return regressions this is unlikely to be the case for four interrelated reasons:

1. **Serial Correlation in the Regression Scores, $x_t e_{t,t+h}$:** Even for one-period-ahead ($h = 1$) predictive regressions, there could be serial correlation in the regression scores, $x_t e_{t,t+h}$, which requires adjustments to $\text{SE}(\widehat{\beta}_i^{(h)})$. The most common approach taken is to use the Newey and West (1987) variance estimator or other heteroskedasticity and autocorrelation consistent/robust (HAC/HAR) estimators such as those proposed in Lazarus et al. (2018).[1]

---

[1] For a textbook treatment of inference in time-series regressions, see Section 14 of Hansen (2022).

2. **Overlapping Nature of Returns:** Even if $e_{t,t+1}$ is serially uncorrelated, there will be serial correlation in $e_{t,t+h}$ for $h > 1$. Furthermore, as h grows and returns are earned over longer holding periods, the left-hand-side variable becomes increasingly persistent (e.g., Valkanov, 2003).
3. **Endogeneity of the Predictors:** It is common in predictive regressions that innovations to the predictors are correlated with the regression errors, $e_{t,t+h}$. For example, if the x_t were generated from a vector autoregression of order one (VAR(1)),

$$x_t = \mu + \Phi x_{t-1} + \eta_t, \qquad (1.3)$$

then it is often the case that the correlation between elements of η_t and $e_{t,t+h}$ is nonzero and possibly large in magnitude (e.g., Stambaugh, 1999).
4. **High Persistence of the Predictors:** Many candidate predictors for future asset returns display very high degrees of serial correlation. For example, if the x_t followed a VAR(1) as in equation (1.3), this would translate into at least one eigenvalue of Φ that is close to one. This requires alternative (nonstandard) asymptotic frameworks for credible inference (e.g., Campbell & Yogo, 2006; Cavanagh, Elliott, & Stock, 1995; Kostakis, Magdalinos, & Stamatogiannis (2014).

These challenges[2] have spurred a number of different approaches to improve inference including the use of resampling procedures. For finite-maturity assets such as bonds, Bauer and Hamilton (2018) and Giglio and Kelly (2017) suggested parametric resampling procedures, whereas, for equity markets, it is common to bootstrap under the null of no predictability.

An alternative approach with better finite sample properties was pioneered in Crump and Gospodinov (2025a) who introduced a novel nonparametric resampling procedure for the nominal yield curve. In the contents of this Element, we build off of this approach and extend the procedure along several dimensions and to other asset classes. Before doing so, we will start with a brief review of the statistical foundations of resampling-based inference.

1.2 A Short Review of Resampling Procedures

Resampling procedures have a long history in the economics and finance literature. For example, Cowles (1933) devised an ingenious approach to evaluate the statistical significance of different trading strategies by randomly reshuffling cards representing possible investment decisions. The most widely

---

[2] For simulation evidence on the extent of the distortions to inference that can occur in this setting, see, for example, Mankiw and Shapiro (1985, 1986) or Ferson, Sarkissian, and Simin (2003).

applicable resampling technique is the "bootstrap," which was formally introduced in Efron (1979) (see, e.g., Hall (1992) or Horowitz (2001) for general treatments).

Describing the bootstrap is most easily done via an example. Suppose we observe a random sample $\{x_t : t = 1, \ldots, T\}$, that is, each x_t is independent and identically distributed (*i.i.d.*) following some distribution with mean θ. A natural estimator of θ is the sample mean, denoted by $\widehat{\theta}$. To conduct inference on θ we require knowledge of the sampling distribution of our estimator, that is, the distribution of $\widehat{\theta} - \theta$. How can we approximate this distribution? Suppose we randomly sample, with replacement, from the x_t to generate a "new" sample (a bootstrap sample or bootstrap draw) of size T, represented as $(x_1^*, \ldots, x_T^*)$, from the original data and calculate the corresponding sample mean, $\widehat{\theta}^*$. As an example, for $T = 6$ we might obtain

$$(x_1^*, x_2^*, x_3^*, x_4^*, x_5^*, x_6^*) = (x_2, x_6, x_1, x_3, x_3, x_5), \quad \widehat{\theta}^* = \frac{1}{6}\sum_{i=1}^{6} x_i^*. \tag{1.4}$$

We can repeat this step B times to obtain B bootstrap samples.

The bootstrap principle states that, under regularity conditions, the distribution of $\widehat{\theta} - \theta$ may be approximated by the distribution of $\widehat{\theta}^* - \widehat{\theta}$ with the degree of approximation improving with the sample size, T, and the number of bootstrap samples, B. The bootstrap principle can also be applied to test statistics rather than the centered estimator, $\widehat{\theta} - \theta$. Let $\text{SE}(\widehat{\theta})$ be the standard error estimate of $\widehat{\theta}$ using the original sample and let $\text{SE}(\widehat{\theta}^*)$ denote its bootstrap analog. Then, the bootstrap principle states that, under regularity conditions, the distribution of the sample t-statistic, $\widehat{t}$, may be approximated by the distribution of the bootstrapped t-statistic, $\widehat{t}^*$, where

$$\widehat{t} = \frac{\widehat{\theta} - \theta}{\text{SE}(\widehat{\theta})} \quad \text{and} \quad \widehat{t}^* = \frac{\widehat{\theta}^* - \widehat{\theta}}{\text{SE}(\widehat{\theta}^*)}. \tag{1.5}$$

A fundamental choice when implementing the bootstrap is whether to impose the null hypothesis in each bootstrap sample. Throughout this monograph, we choose *not* to impose the null hypothesis in our bootstrap samples: a choice that has two advantages. First, imposing the null may compromise the power of the resultant test. Second, even in simple setups, imposing the null hypothesis may lead to an inconsistent bootstrap procedure (e.g., Singh, 1981).

Resampling with replacement is sufficient when the data are *i.i.d.* but requires adjustments when there is dependence across observations which is typically the case in economic and financial data. In these settings, there are two main approaches. First is a parametric bootstrap, in which an assumption is made on the process that describes the evolution of the data, $\{x_t : t = 1 \ldots, T\}$. The following provides an example of a parametric bootstrap.

Example 1 *Suppose $x_t \in \mathbb{R}^q$ follows the VAR(1) from equation (1.3). We can estimate the parameters with OLS to obtain*

$$x_t = \widehat{\mu} + \widehat{\Phi} x_{t-1} + \widehat{\eta}_t. \tag{1.6}$$

We sample, with replacement, from $\{\widehat{\eta}_t : t = 2, \ldots, T\}$ to obtain the bootstrap series $\{\widehat{\eta}_t^* : t = 2, \ldots, T\}$. Using the OLS parameter estimates, and a choice of initial condition x_1^* (e.g., $x_1^* = x_1$), we can build a bootstrapped sample recursively via

$$x_t^* = \widehat{\mu} + \widehat{\Phi} x_{t-1}^* + (\widehat{\eta}_t^* - \overline{\eta}^*), \tag{1.7}$$

where we subtract $\overline{\eta}^* = (T - 1)^{-1} \sum_{s=2}^{T} \widehat{\eta}_s^*$ to ensure that the innovations in each bootstrap sample have a sample mean of zero. Using the data $\{x_t^* : t = 1, \ldots, T\}$ we can construct, in each bootstrap sample, OLS estimates of μ and Φ and label them $\widehat{\mu}^*$ and $\widehat{\Phi}^*$.

The main drawback to the parametric bootstrap approach is that the model might be misspecified, which could lead to incorrect inference. To allow for a general class of models, we can instead directly bootstrap the data, provided the true model is stationary and ergodic, by a nonparametric *block* bootstrap (e.g., Fitzenberger, 1998; Künsch, 1989). To illustrate how to perform a block bootstrap, let us write the data, x_t, in the following stacked form:

$$Z = \begin{bmatrix} x_{1,1} & x_{2,1} & x_{3,1} & \cdots & x_{q,1} \\ x_{1,2} & x_{2,2} & x_{3,2} & \cdots & x_{q,2} \\ \vdots & \vdots & \vdots & & \vdots \\ x_{1,t} & x_{2,t} & x_{3,t} & \cdots & x_{q,t} \\ \vdots & \vdots & \vdots & & \vdots \\ x_{1,T} & x_{2,T} & x_{3,T} & \cdots & x_{q,T} \end{bmatrix}.$$

The bootstrap samples are obtained by drawing, with replacement, blocks of size M rows from the matrix Z, jointly for all cross-sectional observations, where $1 \leq M < T$. Let z_t' be the t-th row of the data matrix Z earlier. Here $z_t = x_t$, but in later chapters, Z will include a collection of different variables in each column. Blocks of size M may be defined as $Z_{t,M} = (z_t, z_{t+1}, \ldots, z_{t+M-1})$ and we resample with replacement k blocks from $(Z_{1,M}, Z_{2,M}, \ldots, Z_{T-M+1,M})$

where k is the smallest integer such that $kM > T$. Then, the bootstrap sample is given by the first T rows[3] of

$$Z^* = \left[(z_1^*, z_2^*, \ldots, z_M^*), (z_{M+1}^*, z_{M+2}^*, \ldots, z_{2M}^*), \ldots \right.$$
$$\left. \ldots, (z_{kM-M+1}^*, z_{kM-M+2}^*, \ldots, z_{kM}^*)\right]'.$$

Unlike the parametric bootstrap approach, the nonparametric block bootstrap is robust to model misspecification as it is agnostic to the true dependence structure of the data. One drawback is that the performance may be sensitive to the choice of M. Since we rely on the block bootstrap throughout this monograph, we will provide guidance on the choice of M tailored to each asset pricing setup.

What if x_t are highly persistent, as is the case, for example, with bond yields or forward rates? We cannot directly block bootstrap such variables because very large block sizes are required to capture the strong dependence across time.[4] This is where the novelty of our approach lies. In each of the different asset pricing settings we consider, we avoid directly resampling highly persistent variables such as the short-term interest rate or the dividend-price ratio, but instead resample primitive objects with weaker dependence properties and reconstruct all necessary variables using economic identities. Importantly, these identities recover and retain the dependence in the original processes without any parametric assumptions about the type and magnitude of this dependence.

At times, however, we will need to bootstrap some mildly persistent series such as macroeconomic variables. In this case, we "pre-whiten" these series using a convenient choice of time-series model, block bootstrap the resulting residuals, and then "re-whiten" them with the estimated model parameters. We can demonstrate this by revisiting Example 1:

Example 2 *We again use a VAR(1) model, but we are no longer assuming that it represents the true data-generating process. Instead it will only serve to reduce the degree of dependence in the objects we bootstrap. We can again rely on equation (1.6) using the OLS estimates to obtain the estimated residuals. This is the pre-whitening step. However, instead of treating $\widehat{\eta}_t$ as if they are estimates of a serially uncorrelated innovation, we block bootstrap them as the first $T - 1$ elements of*

---

[3] Since Z^* is a $kM \times q$ matrix we take the first T rows so that our bootstrap sample is the same length as the data.

[4] See Lahiri (2003) for a comprehensive treatment of resampling methods with dependent data.

$$\widehat{\eta}^* = [(\widehat{\eta}_1^*, \widehat{\eta}_2^*, \ldots, \widehat{\eta}_M^*), (\widehat{\eta}_{M+1}^*, \widehat{\eta}_{M+2}^*, \ldots, \widehat{\eta}_{2M}^*), \ldots$$
$$\ldots, (\widehat{\eta}_{kM-M+1}^*, \widehat{\eta}_{kM-M+2}^*, \ldots, \widehat{\eta}_{kM}^*)]'.$$

Then, we can use the OLS parameter estimates and a choice of initial condition x_1^* (e.g., $x_1^* = x_1$) to build the bootstrapped sample, $\{x_t^* : t = 1, \ldots, T\}$, recursively via equation (1.7). This is the re-whitening step.

Importantly, the model used for pre-whitening is allowed to be misspecified and the remaining degree of dependence is handled by the block bootstrap.[5] This is an example of the hybrid bootstrap of Davison and Hinkley (1997) and Niebuhr, Kreiss, and Paparoditis (2017).

We can now revisit the predictive regression in equation (1.1). One might ask why we don't stack the data as Z with $z_t = (\text{RET}_{t,t+h}, x_t')'$ and follow the same block bootstrap procedure to obtain a bootstrapped sample for $z_t^* = (\text{RET}_{t,t+h}^*, x_t^{*'})'$? Or perhaps pre-whiten the x_t, stack the data as Z with $z_t = (\text{RET}_{t,t+h}, \widehat{\eta}_t')'$, and re-whiten to obtain the bootstrapped sample? The fundamental problem with taking this generic resampling approach to predictive return regressions is that some elements of the x_t are generally a function of the same underlying asset price data and are, thus, linked by economic identities. For a bootstrap procedure to best mimic the behavior of the observed data, these identities should also hold in each bootstrapped sample. This is an issue that has been overlooked outside of Crump and Gospodinov (2025a) but will serve as a common thread throughout this monograph.

To see this clearly, consider the case of predicting stock returns with valuation ratios. The gross equity return is defined as

$$1 + R_{t+1} = \frac{P_{t+1}}{P_t} + \frac{D_{t+1}}{P_t}, \tag{1.8}$$

where P_t is the observed price of the stock at time t and D_t is the associated dividend. The second term on the right-hand side, D_{t+1}/P_t, is the dividend yield at time $t + 1$. A common implementation of the predictive regression given by equation (1.1) sets $r_{t+1}^{(1)} = \log(1 + R_{t+1})$ and $x_{t+1} = \log(D_{t+1}/P_t)$, where $\log(\cdot)$ denotes the natural logarithm. However, any generic resampling procedure, such as those discussed in the previous paragraph, will result in bootstrapped objects such that

$$1 + R_{t+1}^* \neq \frac{P_{t+1}^*}{P_t^*} + \frac{D_{t+1}^*}{P_t^*}. \tag{1.9}$$

---

[5] For additional discussion on the role of pre-whitening in this context, see Crump and Gospodinov (2025a), and for a formal treatment, see Andrews (1991).

In contrast, in Section 4, we introduce a novel bootstrap procedure that uses equity market identities to discipline the resampled data and construct all of the relevant variables in an internally consistent manner so that equation (1.8) holds exactly in each bootstrapped sample. Moreover, we follow the same broad approach in Section 2, where we focus on the nominal yield curve, and in Section 3, where we jointly study the nominal and real yield curves. This is the identity-based resampling approach that we advance in this monograph.

Each section includes a number of figures and tables based on actual asset price data along with simulated data. All of these figures and tables can be reproduced exactly using our companion MATLAB replication package.[6] Finally, required notation is introduced, as needed, throughout the text and summarized on page 79 for reference.

2 Nominal Yield Curves

The nominal yield curve, also known as the term structure of interest rates, plays a key role in modern macroeconomic and financial models. It represents a market price for the time value of money, which serves as an anchor to all other asset prices. Furthermore, it is the linchpin of the monetary policy transmission mechanism. The dominant modeling paradigm for the term structure of interest rates is to rely on parametric models, taking an explicit stand on the cross-sectional and time-series properties of the data. In contrast, the resampling approach introduced in this section, based on Crump and Gospodinov (2025a), aims to be much more flexible, allowing for general dependence in both dimensions. Importantly, this bootstrap approach is agnostic about the true factor structure that generated the data.

2.1 Notation and Properties of the Data

We begin this section by introducing key definitions and notation related to the nominal yield curve. Define $p_t^{(n)}$ as the time t log price of a zero-coupon bond with n periods to maturity that pays \$1 at time $t+n$, where $t=1,\ldots,T$ and $n=1,\ldots,N$. The corresponding log yield is denoted by $y_t^{(n)}$ and satisfies $p_t^{(n)} = -n y_t^{(n)}$. The log forward rate corresponding to a one-period investment between $t+n-1$ and $t+n$, $f_t^{(n)}$, is defined as

$$f_t^{(n)} := p_t^{(n-1)} - p_t^{(n)}. \tag{2.1}$$

---

[6] The companion MATLAB replication package is available at https://github.com/rkcrump/replication-CG_2025_ResamplingAssetPrices.

Since $p_t^{(0)} = 0$, the one-period rate, $y_t^{(1)}$, may equivalently be written as $f_t^{(1)}$. Using the recursive (in n) nature of equation (2.1) and the definition of yields, we have

$$p_t^{(n)} = -\sum_{i=1}^{n} f_t^{(i)}, \qquad y_t^{(n)} = \frac{1}{n}\sum_{i=1}^{n} f_t^{(i)}. \qquad (2.2)$$

We observe that $p_t^{(n)}$ and $y_t^{(n)}$ are cross-sectional partial sums and partial averages of forward rates, respectively. These formulas demonstrate that two prices, $p_t^{(n_1)}$ and $p_t^{(n_2)}$, or two yields, $y_t^{(n_1)}$ and $y_t^{(n_2)}$, have $\min(n_1, n_2)$ forwards in common. This overlap, which arises solely from these term-structure identities, implies differential behavior in the covariance or correlation matrix of forwards relative to yields (or prices). Crump and Gospodinov (2022b) show that this has important implications for studying the factor structure in the yield curve which we discuss later.

Forwards and yields exhibit high time-series persistence which complicates estimation and inference. A popular approach, then, is to, when possible, work with bond returns rather than bond prices or yields. Define the one-period holding return on a bond of maturity n from time t to $t+1$ as

$$r_{t,t+1}^{(n)} := p_{t+1}^{(n-1)} - p_t^{(n)}. \qquad (2.3)$$

The corresponding excess return (in excess of the one-period nominal interest rate) is then

$$rx_{t,t+1}^{(n)} := r_{t,t+1}^{(n)} - y_t^{(1)} = r_{t,t+1}^{(n)} - r_{t,t+1}^{(1)}. \qquad (2.4)$$

The notation $r_{t,t+1}^{(n)}$ and $rx_{t,t+1}^{(n)}$ signifies that these returns are earned from period t to $t+1$. In the sequel, we will simplify notation to $r_{t+1}^{(n)}$ and $rx_{t+1}^{(n)}$, respectively.

Figure 1 presents the time-series properties for these key objects using quarterly data from Gürkaynak, Sack, and Wright (2007). This figure shows clearly that nominal yields and forwards exhibit a high degree of time-series persistence, including a clear downward trend over most of the sample (both displayed in annualized percentage terms). As implied by equation (2.2), yields display a more rigid cross-sectional structure than forwards. The bottom row of Figure 1 shows the time series for nominal returns and the returns in excess of the 3-month (1-quarter) yield. We first observe that returns exhibit only weak serial correlation. This comes about because yields are highly persistent and returns are approximately the time difference of yields. However, returns for bonds with shorter maturities (which tend to be smaller in magnitude) show more meaningful serial correlation. This is no longer the case once we consider excess returns as shown in the bottom right chart. Finally, we note that bond returns exhibit substantial volatility but without a strong cyclical pattern.

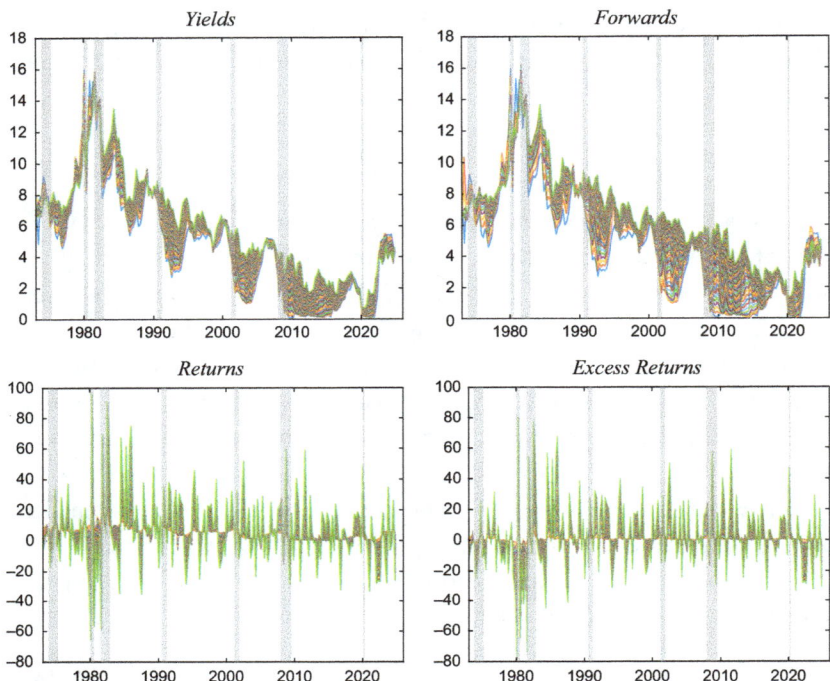

Figure 1 Nominal Yields and Returns. This figure shows the time series of nominal yields and forwards (top row) along with nominal returns and excess nominal returns (bottom row) for maturities up to 40 quarters (in percent, annualized). The sample period is 1973Q1–2024Q4 using quarterly data from Gürkaynak, Sack, and Wright (2007). Grey shaded areas denote NBER recessions.

Figure 1 also shows that bond returns retain a rigid cross-sectional structure similar to yields. This comes about because the overlapping nature of prices relative to forward rates is directly inherited by returns. We can demonstrate this in a straightforward way by defining the return on the following long/short trading strategy: buy an n-maturity bond and short an $(n-1)$-maturity bond ("difference return"),

$$dr_{t+1}^{(n)} := r_{t+1}^{(n)} - r_{t+1}^{(n-1)} = f_t^{(n)} - f_{t+1}^{(n-1)}. \tag{2.5}$$

Then, it follows immediately that excess returns are a partial sum (along maturity) of $dr_{t+1}^{(i)}$,

$$rx_{t+1}^{(n)} = \sum_{i=2}^{n} dr_{t+1}^{(i)}. \tag{2.6}$$

Furthermore, forward rates and difference returns can be related by the following identity,

$$f_t^{(n)} = f_t^{(n)} + f_{t-1}^{(n+1)} - f_{t-1}^{(n+1)} + \cdots + f_{t-N+n}^{(N)} - f_{t-N+n}^{(N)}$$
$$= f_{t-N+n}^{(N)} - \left(f_{t-1}^{(n+1)} - f_t^{(n)}\right) - \left(f_{t-2}^{(n+2)} - f_{t-1}^{(n+1)}\right) - \cdots$$
$$\cdots - \left(f_{t-N+n}^{(N)} - f_{t-N+n+1}^{(N-1)}\right)$$
$$= f_{t-N+n}^{(N)} - dr_t^{(n+1)} - dr_{t-1}^{(n+2)} - \cdots - dr_{t-N+n+1}^{(N)}. \quad (2.7)$$

In particular, the relation between forwards across time informs the relations between future returns and the current term structure. Equation (2.7) implies that if we observe the longest horizon forward rate, $\left\{f_t^{(N)}\right\}_{t=2}^T$, all difference returns, $\left\{(dr_t^{(2)}, \ldots, dr_t^{(N)})\right\}_{t=2}^T$, along with an initial forward curve, $\left(f_1^{(1)}, \ldots, f_1^{(N)}\right)$, we are able to construct the entire forward curve $\left\{\left(f_t^{(1)}, \ldots, f_t^{(N)}\right)\right\}_{t=1}^T$ and yield curve $\left\{\left(y_t^{(1)}, \ldots, y_t^{(N)}\right)\right\}_{t=1}^T$.[7]

2.1.1 Time-Series Properties of Bond Data

In this subsection, we demonstrate the appealing time-series and cross-sectional properties of difference returns, $dr_t^{(n)}$, as a primitive object for resampling. First, yields and forwards are not well-suited for direct resampling due to their strong time-series and cross-sectional dependence. But what about resampling the first-differenced yields $\Delta y_t^{(n)}$? To illustrate why this may not be desirable, we assume that the one-period yield (short rate) follows an AR(1) process (e.g., Vašíček, 1977)

$$y_{t+1}^{(1)} = \rho y_t^{(1)} + \varsigma_{t+1}, \quad (2.8)$$

where $|\rho| < 1$ and ς_{t+1} is an innovation term with $\mathbb{E}_t[\varsigma_{t+1}] = 0$ and $\mathbb{E}_t[\varsigma_{t+1}^2] = \sigma^2$. Here, $\mathbb{E}_t[\cdot]$ denotes the conditional expectation based on the information set available at time t, $\mathcal{F}_t$. Since

$$\Delta y_{t+1}^{(1)} := y_{t+1}^{(1)} - y_t^{(1)}$$
$$= (\rho - 1)y_t^{(1)} + \varsigma_{t+1}$$
$$= \varsigma_{t+1} + (\rho - 1)\varsigma_t + (\rho - 1)\rho\varsigma_{t-1} + (\rho - 1)\rho^2\varsigma_{t-2} + \cdots, \quad (2.9)$$

then $\Delta y_{t+1}^{(1)}$ has an infinite moving average representation that poses difficulties to resampling the differenced data effectively. Furthermore, $\Delta y_t^{(n)}$ retains the strong cross-sectional dependence in the original yields $y_t^{(n)}$ across n.

---

[7] For $t \leq N + 1$, we can obtain forwards by directly relying on the recursive relationship, $f_t^{(n)} = f_{t-1}^{(n+1)} - dr_t^{(n+1)}$.

Interestingly, the differenced returns do not suffer from this problem. To see this, assume that the expectations hypothesis holds which implies

$$f_t^{(n)} = \alpha^{(n)} + \mathbb{E}_t[y_{t+n-1}^{(1)}], \qquad (2.10)$$

where $\alpha^{(n)}$ is a constant bond premium. By backward substitution of equation (2.8), we have $y_{t+n}^{(1)} = \rho^n y_t^{(1)} + \sum_{i=0}^{n-1} \rho^i \varsigma_{t+n-i}$. Then, substituting for $y_{t+n-1}^{(1)}$ in equation (2.10) and evaluating the conditional expectation gives

$$f_t^{(n)} = \alpha^{(n)} + \rho^{n-1} y_t^{(1)}. \qquad (2.11)$$

Similarly,

$$\begin{aligned} f_{t+1}^{(n-1)} &= \alpha^{(n-1)} + \rho^{n-2} y_{t+1}^{(1)} \\ &= \alpha^{(n-1)} + \rho^{n-1} y_t^{(1)} + \rho^{n-2} \varsigma_{t+1}. \end{aligned} \qquad (2.12)$$

Substituting these expressions for $f_t^{(n)}$ and $f_{t+1}^{(n-1)}$ into equation (2.5), we may express the difference return as

$$dr_{t+1}^{(n)} = [\alpha^{(n)} - \alpha^{(n-1)}] - \rho^{n-2} \varsigma_{t+1}. \qquad (2.13)$$

Thus, $dr_{t+1}^{(n)}$ inherits the serial correlation properties of ς_{t+1} and the degree of persistence in the yields (characterized by ρ) does not affect the time-series properties of the bootstrapped primitive object $dr_{t+1}^{(n)}$. To repeat, this is not the case if the primitive object for the resampling is either $y_{t+1}^{(1)}$ or $\Delta y_{t+1}^{(1)}$. Intuitively, $dr_{t+1}^{(n)}$ involves an additional cross-sectional difference and exploits the "cointegration" between the two adjacent forward rates that immunizes the process to the specific persistence of the individual forward rates. Importantly, however, this persistence is restored by reconstructing the forward rates via the identity in equation (2.7). More generally, if we allow for a time-varying risk premium, the term $\alpha_t^{(n)} - \alpha_t^{(n-1)}$ will introduce another source of time-series dependence that motivates the block bootstrapping scheme for $dr_{t+1}^{(n)}$.

2.1.2 Cross-Sectional Properties of Bond Data

As we saw in Figure 1, bond data are characterized by strong dependence in the time-series *and* the cross-sectional dimension. The difficulties of dealing with highly persistent time-series data are, by now, well established in the existing literature. However, Crump and Gospodinov (2022b) show how, in this setting, cross-sectional dependence can pose unique challenges to accurately determining the minimal dimension of the drivers of the term structure. We can illustrate this point using a simplified example from Crump and Gospodinov (2022b).

We stack excess returns and difference returns in the $(N-1) \times T$ matrices X^{rx} and X^{dr}, respectively. Then, equation (2.6) implies

$$X^{rx} = \mathsf{L}_{N-1} X^{dr} \quad \text{or} \quad X^{dr} = \mathsf{L}_{N-1}^{-1} X^{rx}, \tag{2.14}$$

where L_{N-1} is a $(N-1) \times (N-1)$ lower triangular matrix of ones. Thus, difference returns and excess returns are related by a simple nonsingular transformation. The covariance matrix of X^{rx} is $V_{X,rx} = \mathsf{L}_{N-1} V_{X,dr} \mathsf{L}'_{N-1}$, where $V_{X,dr}$ is the covariance matrix of X^{dr}.

For simplicity, assume that $V_{X,dr} = \sigma^2 \cdot \mathsf{I}_{N-1}$, where I_{N-1} denotes the $(N-1) \times (N-1)$ identity matrix, so that $V_{X,rx} = \sigma^2 \cdot \mathsf{L}_{N-1} \mathsf{L}'_{N-1}$. Principal components analysis (PCA) is commonly based on the eigendecomposition of $V_{X,rx}$. Notice that, here, difference returns are driven by a primitive process of dimension $N-1$ rather than the typical assumption of a small number of underlying factors. However, the factor structure is extracted from excess returns that exhibit strong cross-sectional dependence due to the overlapping maturities in adjacent excess returns. To see this, note that by equation (2.6), excess returns of maturities n_1 and n_2 will have $\min(n_1, n_2) - 1$ difference returns in common.

The factor loadings are the eigenvectors $\psi_j = (\psi_{1,j}, \ldots, \psi_{N-1,j})'$ of matrix $V_{X,rx}$. In this example, they are given by

$$\psi_{\ell,j} = \frac{2}{\sqrt{2N-1}} \sin\left(\frac{\ell(2j-1)\pi}{2N-1}\right) \tag{2.15}$$

for $\ell = 1, \ldots, N-1$ and $j = 1, \ldots, N-1$. Note that the shape of these factor loadings is fully characterized by the order of the corresponding eigenvector, j, and the maximum maturity, N. Despite the simplicity and unrealistic nature of the design, Figure 2 shows that these analytical factor loadings mimic closely the highly structured polynomial pattern in the PC loadings for excess returns in the data. In this example, the ordered eigenvalues of the $V_{X,rx}$ matrix can be expressed as

$$\lambda_j = \frac{\sigma^2}{2 - 2\cos\left(\frac{(2j-1)\pi}{2N-1}\right)}, \quad \lambda_1 > \lambda_2 > \cdots > \lambda_{N-1}, \tag{2.16}$$

which, again, are only a function of j and N. Figure 2 shows that the first three eigenvalues, λ_1, λ_2, and λ_3, account for more than 93% of the sum of the eigenvalues (which is equal to $(N-1)N/2$).

The key takeaway from this example is that when $V_{X,dr} \propto \mathsf{I}_{N-1}$, there are $N-1$ idiosyncratic factors that are driving bond returns; however, standard outputs from PCA suggest a much smaller dimension of the factor space.

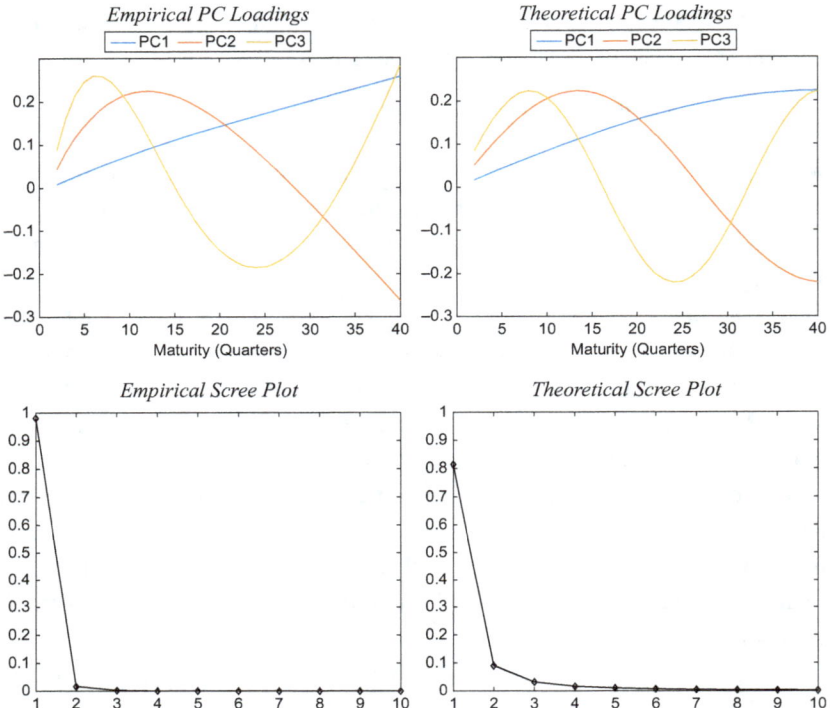

Figure 2 Empirical and Theoretical Principal Component Loadings of Bond Returns. The left column of this figure presents the first three principal component (PC) loadings for excess returns and the associated scree plot based on an eigendecomposition of the sample covariance matrix. The sample period is 1973Q1–2024Q4 using quarterly data from Gürkaynak, Sack, and Wright (2007). The right column shows the theoretical counterparts based on equations (2.15) and (2.16).

The intuition for this result is that the overlapping sum, which links difference returns and excess returns, induces strong cross-sectional correlations that the PCA method interprets as evidence of only a small number of underlying factors. Crump and Gospodinov (2022b) provide further evidence with more realistic setups, but the same conclusion applies: namely, that pinning down the dimension of the factor space is extremely challenging. Thus, it would be preferable to avoid committing to a tightly parameterized, finite-dimensional factor structure that may result in the omission of important information embedded in the yield curve.[8] This insight informs our resampling approach.

---

[8] Crump and Gospodinov (2022b) show that committing to a low-dimensional parametric structure can result in large hedging and portfolio allocation errors (see also Filipović, Pelger, & Ye, 2024).

2.2 A Nonparametric Bootstrap

Crump and Gospodinov (2025a) introduce a general bootstrap framework relying on the identity from equation (2.7). In practice, many yield curve datasets have gaps in the available maturities, and so we follow the modified bootstrap approach from Crump and Gospodinov (2025a). Before proceeding, it will be useful to define $f_t^{(n,h)}$ as the log forward rate corresponding to an h-period investment between $t+n-h$ and $t+n$

$$f_t^{(n,h)} := p_t^{(n-h)} - p_t^{(n)}, \qquad f_t^{(n)} =: f_t^{(n,1)}. \qquad (2.17)$$

Suppose we observe the monthly prices of zero-coupon bonds with maturities ranging from one to ten years, $\left(p_t^{(12)}, p_t^{(24)} \ldots, p_t^{(120)}\right)$. We can then construct

$$\begin{aligned}
z_{1,t} &= p_t^{(108)} - p_t^{(120)} \\
z_{2,t} &= p_t^{(96)} - p_t^{(108)} - \left(p_{t-1}^{(108)} - p_{t-1}^{(120)}\right) \\
z_{3,t} &= p_t^{(84)} - p_t^{(96)} - \left(p_{t-1}^{(96)} - p_{t-1}^{(108)}\right) \\
&\vdots \\
z_{9,t} &= p_t^{(12)} - p_t^{(24)} - \left(p_{t-1}^{(24)} - p_{t-1}^{(36)}\right) \\
z_{10,t} &= p_t^{(0)} - p_t^{(12)} - \left(p_{t-1}^{(12)} - p_{t-1}^{(24)}\right).
\end{aligned} \qquad (2.18)$$

Furthermore, $z_{1,t}$ through $z_{10,t}$ can also be written in terms of forward rates, so that

$$\begin{aligned}
z_{1,t} &= f_t^{(120,12)} \\
z_{2,t} &= f_t^{(108,12)} - f_{t-1}^{(120,12)} \\
z_{3,t} &= f_t^{(96,12)} - f_{t-1}^{(108,12)} \\
&\vdots \\
z_{9,t} &= f_t^{(24,12)} - f_{t-1}^{(36,12)} \\
z_{10,t} &= f_t^{(12,12)} - f_{t-1}^{(24,12)}.
\end{aligned} \qquad (2.19)$$

Rather than work directly with $z_{1,t}$, which may be persistent, we instead pre-whiten this series using an AR(1) process as

$$z_{1,t+1} = \hat{\mu} + \hat{\phi} \cdot z_{1,t} + \tilde{z}_{1,t+1}, \qquad (2.20)$$

where $\hat{\mu}$ and $\hat{\phi}$ may be obtained by OLS estimation. Both the pre-whitening step and the bootstrap itself require a choice of initial conditions. Throughout this monograph, we always choose the first observation of the realized data as our initial condition. Alternative time periods or other fixed choices are also valid.

We can then proceed to block bootstrap using the $(T-1)\times 10$ matrix Z^N which has tth row equal to $(\tilde{z}_{1,t+1}, z_{2,t+1} \ldots, z_{10,t+1})$ and reconstruct the entire yield curve through the definitions and identities introduced at the beginning of the section. At first glance, it may seem infeasible to rebuild all yield-curve objects based on only an initial set of prices and the time series of $(\tilde{z}_{1,t}, z_{2,t} \ldots, z_{10,t})$. To see why this can be accomplished, recall that $p_t^{(0)} = 0$ so that we can obtain $p_t^{(12)}$ so long as we observe all prices in the previous period using the identity

$$p_t^{(12)} = -z_{10,t} - \left(p_{t-1}^{(12)} - p_{t-1}^{(24)}\right). \tag{2.21}$$

We can follow the same logic to obtain $p_t^{(24)}$ using $z_{9,t}$, $p_t^{(12)}$, $p_{t-1}^{(24)}$, and $p_{t-1}^{(36)}$. We continue these steps to obtain all ten prices.

The bootstrap algorithm can then be outlined as follows:

Step 1: Block bootstrap Z^N to obtain Z^{N*}.

Step 2: Use equation (2.20) to obtain the bootstrapped time series of $z_{1,t}^*$ for $t = 1, \ldots, T$.

Step 3: Use the recursive relationships given by equation (2.18) to obtain

$$\left(p_t^{(12)*}, p_t^{(24)*} \ldots, p_t^{(120)*}\right), \quad t = 1, \ldots, T,$$

and corresponding bond yields,

$$\left(y_t^{(12)*}, y_t^{(24)*} \ldots, y_t^{(120)*}\right), \quad t = 1, \ldots, T.$$

Step 4: Repeat Steps 1–3 to obtain B bootstrap samples.

To perform Step 1, we need a choice of the block size M. We follow the recommendation in Crump and Gospodinov (2025a) to use

$$M = (TN)^{2/5}, \tag{2.22}$$

where, here, we use monthly data with a maximum maturity of ten years so that $N = 120$.

To implement Step 3 in practice, we start by constructing

$$p_2^{(12)*} = -z_{10,2}^* - (p_1^{(12)} - p_1^{(24)}), \tag{2.23}$$

using the identity given in equation (2.21). Next, we have that

$$p_2^{(24)*} = p_2^{(12)*} - z_{9,2}^* - (p_1^{(24)} - p_1^{(36)}). \tag{2.24}$$

We can continue up to $p_2^{(120)*}$ and then proceed to $t = 3$, where

$$p_3^{(12)*} = -z_{10,3}^* - (p_2^{(12)*} - p_2^{(24)*}). \tag{2.25}$$

Next, we have that

$$p_3^{(24)*} = p_3^{(12)*} - z_{9,3}^* - (p_2^{(24)*} - p_2^{(36)*}), \qquad (2.26)$$

and so on for $t > 3$. Following Steps 1–3 then produces a single bootstrap draw of the nominal yield curve. In practice, we can implement the bootstrap without using prices and relying only on forward rates and yields (see equation (2.17)). When doing so, as a convention, we always work with these objects in annualized percentage terms.

In some applications, such as predictive return regressions, one may want to jointly resample the yield curve with an external set of variables. Let w_t represent these additional variables. Then, we can modify the bootstrap earlier by pre-whitening using a VAR(1) to accommodate the additional variables

$$\begin{pmatrix} z_{1,t+1} \\ w_{t+1} \end{pmatrix} = \hat{\mu} + \hat{\Phi} \begin{pmatrix} z_{1,t} \\ w_t \end{pmatrix} + \begin{pmatrix} \tilde{z}_{1,t+1} \\ \tilde{w}_{t+1} \end{pmatrix}, \qquad (2.27)$$

where $\hat{\mu}$ and $\hat{\Phi}$ may be obtained from OLS estimation. With additional variables, Steps 1 and 3 remain the same, and in Step 2 we construct the time series of $z_{1,t}^*$ and w_t^* using equation (2.27) by re-whitening.[9]

Remark 1 *Throughout the monograph, we will rely on a VAR(1) model when we pre-whiten the data. At times, it can be beneficial to perform bias correction of the OLS estimator when Φ has a maximum eigenvalue close to one. We do not bias correct these parameters in any of the results in this monograph as Crump and Gospodinov (2025a) showed that the implications for inference are negligible. If bias correction is deemed necessary, we recommend the bootstrap bias correction of Φ, proposed in Kilian (1998), that is utilized in Crump and Gospodinov (2025a).* □

Remark 2 *An additional possible modification to the bootstrap is to adjust for the yield-level dependence of volatility which was suggested by Rebonato and Zanetti (2023). Specifically, as shown in Rebonato and El Aouadi (2021) (see also Rebonato, 2023), there is a well-behaved one-to-one relation between the level and volatility of yields. Rebonato and Zanetti (2023) recommend exploiting this relationship by first transforming the observed yields to undo this relation (producing "disguised" yields which are approximately homoskedastic). Using these transformed yields, the bootstrap can then be implemented as in Steps 1–3 earlier to obtain a bootstrap sample of*

---

[9] Note that we first demean $\tilde{z}_{1,t+1}$ and $\tilde{w}_{t+1}$, before re-whitening the bootstrapped data.

disguised yields. Then, these bootstrapped yields are re-transformed ("undisguised") to reestablish the relation between the level and volatility of yields. The benefits of this modification are shown in Rebonato and Zanetti (2023). □

2.3 Revisiting the "Tent Shape"

To motivate the need for a nonparametric bootstrap tailored to the term structure of interest rates, we revisit the work of Cochrane and Piazzesi (2005, 2008). Cochrane and Piazzesi (2005, 2008) investigate the relation between future one-year holding period returns and the current forward curve which is characterized by a "tent-shape" pattern in the estimated regression coefficients.

Before proceeding, define the excess h-period holding return

$$rx_{t-h,t}^{(n,h)} := r_{t-h,t}^{(n,h)} + p_{t-h}^{(h)}, \tag{2.28}$$

where

$$r_{t-h,t}^{(n,h)} := p_t^{(n-h)} - p_{t-h}^{(n)}, \qquad r_t^{(n)} =: r_{t-1,t}^{(n,1)}. \tag{2.29}$$

The notation $r_{t-h,t}^{(n,h)}$ and $rx_{t-h,t}^{(n,h)}$ signifies that these returns are earned over the h periods from $t-h$ to t. In the sequel, we will simplify notation to $r_t^{(n,h)}$ and $rx_t^{(n,h)}$, respectively, and, in the special case where $h=1$, simply, $r_t^{(n)}$ and $rx_t^{(n)}$.

We follow Cochrane and Piazzesi (2005) and run monthly predictive regressions of excess 12-month holding returns of the form

$$\begin{aligned}rx_{t+12}^{(n,12)} = \alpha^{(n)} &+ \beta_1^{(n)} \cdot y_t^{(12)} + \beta_2^{(n)} \cdot f_t^{(24,12)} + \beta_3^{(n)} \cdot f_t^{(36,12)} \\&+ \beta_4^{(n)} \cdot f_t^{(48,12)} + \beta_5^{(n)} \cdot f_t^{(60,12)} + \varepsilon_{t+12}^{(n,12)},\end{aligned} \tag{2.30}$$

where $n \in \{24, 36, 48, 60\}$.

The black solid line in the left column of Figure 3 exactly replicates the tent-shaped estimated regression coefficients averaged across the four maturities as in Cochrane and Piazzesi (2005) using Fama-Bliss discount bond data over the 1964m1–2003m12 sample period. The black solid line in the right column of the figure replicates the R^2 for each of the four regressions. A candidate resampling procedure should mimic these patterns that are observed in the data. The multi-colored lines in the top row of Figure 3 represent the same estimated quantities but from individual bootstrap replications based on the nonparametric bootstrap we introduced in the previous section. In the top-left chart, we can see that the bootstrap estimates follow a contour similar to the original tent shape. Furthermore, in the top right chart we observe that the pattern of R^2 also shows a distinct kink at the 48-month (4-year) maturity. It is important to emphasize that the nonparametric bootstrap does not take a stand on the factor

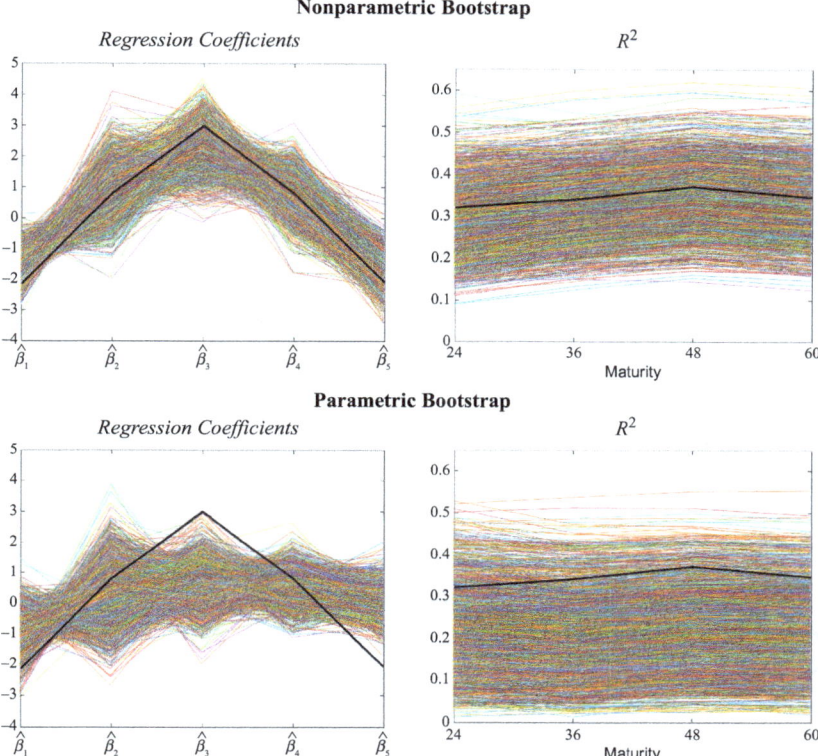

Figure 3 Resampling the Tent Shape of Cochrane and Piazzesi (2005).
This figure shows the results of the nonparametric bootstrap procedure introduced in Section 2.2 as compared to a standard parametric VAR(1) bootstrap of forwards. The regression specification is given in equation (2.30). The sample period is 1964m1–2003m12. The left column presents the sample OLS estimates (black line) and associated bootstrap OLS estimates (multi-colored lines) for $\frac{1}{4} \sum_{n \in \{24,36,48,60\}} (\hat{\beta}_1^{(n)}, \ldots, \hat{\beta}_5^{(n)})$. The right column presents the sample R^2 (black line) and associated bootstrap R^2 estimates (multi-colored lines) across maturities. Bootstrap draws are based on the bootstrap procedure introduced in Section 2.2 using B = 1,999.

structure or the exact time-series dynamics of the data. Despite this, these features in the data, based on estimates of equation (2.30), are preserved in the bootstrapped samples.

As a comparison, we also implement a parametric bootstrap based on a VAR(1) model for $\left(y_t^{(12)}, f_t^{(24,12)}, f_t^{(36,12)}, f_t^{(48,12)}, f_t^{(60,12)}\right)'$ as in Example 1. In the bottom row, we show the corresponding bootstrapped regression coefficients and R^2. In contrast to the nonparametric bootstrap, the parametric alternative fails to capture the pronounced tent shape in the data. Moreover, the parametric bootstrap also misses key features of the regression R², such as the kink, and the bootstrap draws do not appear to be centered at the sample estimate. This is evidence that a rigid parametric structure can fail to replicate the salient properties of the data.

The original work of Cochrane and Piazzesi (2005) has spawned a number of papers studying return prediction based on linear combinations of forwards. It has been established that different yield curve datasets (which are based on different interpolation procedures) produce different shapes of loadings on the coefficients (e.g., Cochrane & Piazzesi, 2004; Dai, Singleton, & Yang, 2004; Rebonato, 2015; Rebonato & Nyholm, 2025). The key issue here, however, is not the specific shape of the loadings in the Fama-Bliss data but that the nonparametric bootstrap reproduces the primary features of these data. Importantly, this is achieved without imposing a specific structure of how the data were generated.

2.4 Simulation Evidence

In this section, we investigate the finite-sample properties of the nonparametric bootstrap using a simulation design inspired by the empirical results of Section 2.3. Let

$$g_t = \left(y_t^{(12)}, f_t^{(24,12)}, f_t^{(36,12)}, f_t^{(48,12)}, f_t^{(60,12)}\right)'. \tag{2.31}$$

Based on the failure of the VAR(1) model to mimic the properties of the data in Figure 3, we assume that g_t follows a VAR(2) to allow for richer dynamic behavior:

$$g_t = \mu_g + \Phi_{g1} \cdot g_{t-1} + \Phi_{g2} \cdot g_{t-2} + \eta_t^g, \tag{2.32}$$

where η_t^g are i.i.d. innovations with variance matrix Σ_η. We calibrate the VAR(2) parameters using OLS estimates based on the Fama-Bliss data over the sample period 1964m1–2003m12. Our calibrated parameters are then $\widetilde{\Phi}_{g1}, \widetilde{\Phi}_{g2}$, and $\widetilde{\Sigma}_\eta$. The calibrated system has a maximum eigenvalue of 0.98 exhibiting a high degree of persistence.

We simulate forwards assuming Gaussian innovations, $\eta_t^g \sim \mathcal{N}\left(0, \widetilde{\Sigma}_\eta\right)$, and using the calibrated autoregressive matrices, $\widetilde{\Phi}_{g1}$ and $\widetilde{\Phi}_{g2}$. Based on the simulated forwards, g_t, we construct simulated yields and returns using equations (2.2), (2.3), and (2.28). We then run regressions of the form

$$rx_{t+12}^{(n,12)} = \alpha^{(n)} + \beta^{(n)\prime} g_t + \varepsilon_{t+12}^{(n,12)}, \tag{2.33}$$

and conduct inference on the elements of $\beta^{(n)}$. Note that with these calibrated parameters and the choice of a VAR(2) model, $\beta^{(n)}$ will have a tent-shape.

Because the true forwards follow a VAR(2), equation (2.33) is misspecified in the sense that the true data-generating process has a linear conditional expectation in terms of g_t and g_{t-1}. We thus view $\beta^{(n)}$ as a projection coefficient only and evaluate the ability of the bootstrap to accommodate this form of misspecification. These results complement those of Crump and Gospodinov (2025a), who present extensive simulation evidence demonstrating the excellent finite-sample properties of the bootstrap under correct specification.

In Section 2.5.3 of the Appendix, we provide detailed information on how to implement the bootstrap methodology for any given dataset. All of our results are based on a sample size of $T = 500$ with $B = 399$ across $5,000$ simulations. The values of the true parameters, $\beta^{(n)}$, can be obtained analytically and are given in Section 2.5.2 of the Appendix. For power, we consider tests of $\mathbb{H}_0$: $\beta_i^{(n)} = 0$, where $\beta_i^{(n)}$ is the ith element of $\beta^{(n)}$. We omit results for the constant term as it is not generally a parameter of interest in these applications.

We compare our bootstrap (labeled "CG") to a number of different alternatives. The first one is an oracle bootstrap that uses the full parametric structure of the data-generating process, including knowledge of the true parameters. The only sampling uncertainty in this method arises from the randomness generated from the $B = 399$ simulated draws of η_t^g. As $B \to \infty$, the oracle procedure, centered at the true parameter value, obtains the exact finite-sample distribution of the t-statistic. Second, we use the conventional Newey and West (1987) variance estimator based on $h = 12$ lags (labeled "NW"). Finally, we also make comparisons to the inference procedures introduced in Lazarus et al. (2018). The first approach uses the equal-weighted cosine (EWC) estimator of the long-run variance and a limiting Student's t distribution (labeled "LLSW-EWC"). The second approach uses the variance estimator of Newey and West (1987) and a fixed-b asymptotic approximation ("LLSW-NW"). In this setup, LLSW-EWC almost uniformly dominates LLSW-NW in terms of size control and so we only report the former in the tables.[10]

Table 1 reports results on the empirical size and power of our bootstrap along with the aforementioned alternative approaches. The nominal levels of the test statistics are all 10%. The left column presents empirical size for t-tests on each of the five coefficients across four different regression specifications corresponding to excess returns of different maturities. The right column reports the associated size-adjusted (SA) power. The top panel shows that the nonparametric bootstrap has empirical size near the nominal level with only some modest under-rejections for the coefficient associated with the second regressor. Despite the excellent size control, we see that the nonparametric bootstrap

---

[10] The full results are available in the MATLAB replication code.

Table 1 Nominal Bond Returns. This table presents empirical size and size-adjusted (SA) power for the predictive regression given by equation (2.33). The nominal level is 10%, and the sample size is $T = 500$. Each column reports results for the t-test associated with the regressor g_{it}, $i \in \{1,\ldots,5\}$. Each row reports results for bond returns of the corresponding maturity. Based on 5,000 simulations and 399 bootstrap replications per simulation.

	CG Bootstrap									
	Size					SA Power				
	g_{1t}	g_{2t}	g_{3t}	g_{4t}	g_{5t}	g_{1t}	g_{2t}	g_{3t}	g_{4t}	g_{5t}
2y	0.095	0.050	0.084	0.081	0.101	0.443	0.448	0.201	0.087	0.276
3y	0.089	0.049	0.085	0.079	0.108	0.403	0.166	0.743	0.103	0.374
4y	0.086	0.051	0.083	0.082	0.106	0.378	0.096	0.601	0.232	0.446
5y	0.082	0.053	0.084	0.086	0.106	0.348	0.071	0.510	0.133	0.161
	Oracle Bootstrap									
	Size					SA Power				
2y	0.106	0.103	0.106	0.102	0.102	0.530	0.456	0.281	0.105	0.274
3y	0.110	0.102	0.106	0.099	0.103	0.499	0.199	0.761	0.118	0.370
4y	0.107	0.103	0.107	0.101	0.102	0.474	0.144	0.629	0.227	0.438
5y	0.105	0.107	0.104	0.101	0.100	0.447	0.124	0.545	0.140	0.169
	Newey-West									
	Size					SA Power				
2y	0.206	0.167	0.168	0.159	0.190	0.517	0.450	0.268	0.102	0.272
3y	0.201	0.170	0.171	0.159	0.192	0.480	0.192	0.753	0.116	0.365
4y	0.199	0.169	0.168	0.158	0.190	0.463	0.137	0.615	0.228	0.436
5y	0.198	0.166	0.170	0.161	0.189	0.433	0.118	0.526	0.139	0.168
	LLSW-EWC									
	Size					SA Power				
2y	0.161	0.133	0.140	0.129	0.145	0.510	0.441	0.261	0.098	0.264
3y	0.154	0.136	0.135	0.129	0.148	0.473	0.193	0.736	0.116	0.361
4y	0.155	0.135	0.134	0.128	0.143	0.452	0.137	0.604	0.222	0.425
5y	0.154	0.137	0.135	0.131	0.146	0.427	0.120	0.513	0.134	0.164

exhibits only minimal loss of power relative to the (infeasible) oracle bootstrap benchmark shown in the second panel.[11] The two methods based on asymptotic approximations (NW and LLSW-EWC) uniformly over-reject the null when the null is true with empirical size always above 10%. The failure of off-the-shelf inference methods to control empirical size underscores the difficulty of conducting trustworthy inference in this setting and the benefits of a tailored bootstrap procedure.[12]

We can also use our nonparametric bootstrap to assess the sampling distribution of other statistics, such as the regression R^2. In Section 2.5.2 of the Appendix we derive the true R^2 associated with equation (2.33) for each maturity n. Of course, in each simulation, s, the regression R^2, denoted by $\widehat{R}^2_{(s)}$, is a random object. The orange bars in Figure 4 show the realized values of $\widehat{R}^2_{(s)}$ for $s = 1, \ldots, 5000$. The black vertical line indicates the population R^2 and so we may conclude that there is an upward bias in finite samples. We can compare the sampling distribution of $\widehat{R}^2_{(s)}$ to its bootstrap counterpart using the "bootstrap principle" introduced in Section 1. Let $\widehat{R}^{2*}_{(s),b}$ be the bth bootstrap estimate for the sth simulation. The blue bars in Figure 4 present a histogram of

$$R^2 + \left(\widehat{R}^{2*}_{(s),b} - \widehat{R}^2_{(s)}\right) \tag{2.34}$$

across $b = 1, \ldots, 399$ and $s = 1, \ldots, 5000$. It is important to reiterate that since we bootstrap all objects at once, we can obtain the requisite statistics for all four maturities considered simultaneously.

We can see from Figure 4 that the bootstrap distribution mimics the degree of variability and the overall shape of the sampling distribution. Moreover, the peak of the distribution is close to the vertical line, indicating that it is approximately centered correctly. This is consistent with the empirical results shown in Figure 3. We can also observe from Figure 4 that the two histograms do not perfectly align. As $T \to \infty$, this discrepancy will vanish and so is solely a manifestation of the limited sample size.

These results are consistent with, and complementary to, the more extensive simulation evidence provided in Crump and Gospodinov (2025a), who clearly demonstrate that the bootstrap approach introduced in Section 2.2 has desirable finite-sample properties and strongly outperforms the existing procedures available in the literature.

---

[11] For some entries in the table, the power of the CG bootstrap exceeds that of the oracle bootstrap. This can arise from either slight relative over-rejections under the null hypothesis or some residual randomness from the limited simulation or bootstrap draws.

[12] We should note that Lazarus et al. (2018) do not recommend the use of their procedures in cases where the data have medium-to-high persistence. However, we include the results here as these approaches are routinely utilized in empirical applications.

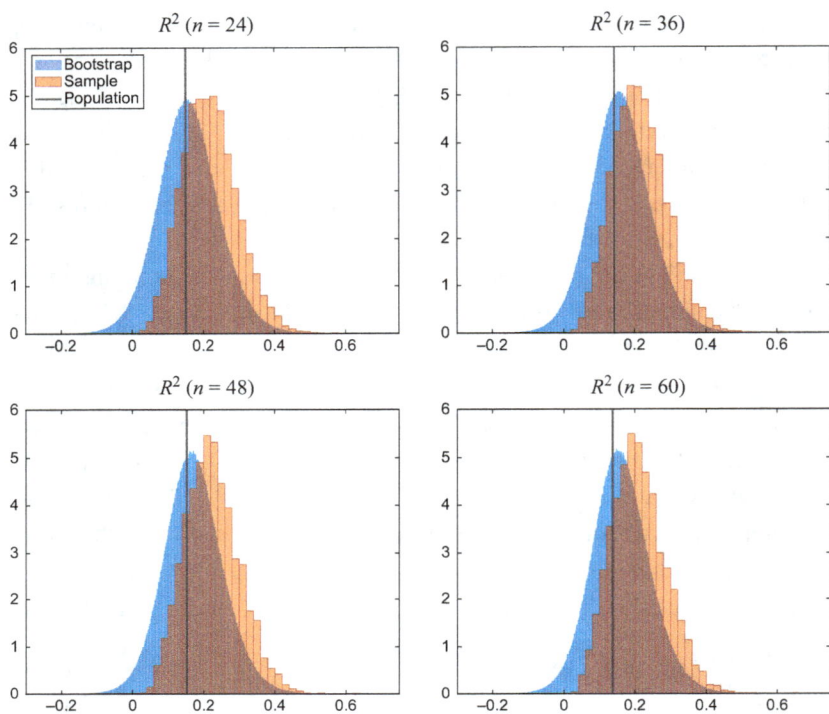

Figure 4 Sampling Distributions of R^2. This figure displays the sampling distribution of the sample R^2 and the bootstrapped R^2 in the simulation design described in the main text. The black vertical line signifies the population R^2. The four charts show the results for the regression specification in equation (2.33) for excess returns of two-year, three-year, four-year, and five-year maturities ($n \in \{24, 36, 48, 60\}$). Based on 5,000 simulations and 399 bootstrap replications per simulation.

Further, the generality of this bootstrap approach allows it to be used in a wide range of applications beyond that presented in Section 2.3. For example, Crump and Gospodinov (2025a) use the bootstrap to revisit the statistical properties of regression-based tests of the expectations hypothesis. They show that the tests, which historically have been relied upon to provide the strongest evidence against the expectations hypothesis, are also the tests with the most variable parameter estimates. As another example, Crump and Gospodinov (2025a) construct bias-corrected estimates and confidence intervals for the probability of recession based on information in the yield curve. The authors show that the direction of the bias correction closely aligns with the impressive forecasting record associated with the term spread and the time-varying informativeness of this relation (see also Crump & Gospodinov, 2025b).

Finally, in an earlier version of the paper, Crump and Gospodinov (2022a) show that a simple measure of tail risk, the spread between the VIX and VXO indices, significantly forecasts future bond returns even after controlling for the information in the current term structure of interest rates.

2.5 Appendix to Section 2

2.5.1 Data Description

In this section, we utilize two different datasets on the zero-coupon yield curve. The first dataset is from Gürkaynak, Sack, and Wright (2007) and is available on the website of the Board of Governors of the Federal Reserve.[13] Quarterly data are constructed as the last available daily observation for each quarter. The second dataset is the Fama-Bliss dataset from Cochrane and Piazzesi (2005) and is available in their replication package.[14] All series used follow the definitions introduced at the beginning of the section.

2.5.2 Additional Details on Simulation Design

To obtain the true parameter value for the regressions in the simulation design, we need to calculate

$$\beta^{(n)} = \mathbb{V}(g_t)^{-1} \mathbb{C}\left(g_t, rx_{t+12}^{(n,12)}\right) = \bar{\Sigma}_{g,11}^{-1} \mathbb{C}\left(g_t, rx_{t+12}^{(n,12)}\right), \qquad (2.35)$$

where $\bar{\Sigma}_{g,11} = [I_5 \ 0_5] \bar{\Sigma}_g [I_5 \ 0_5]'$, 0_5 is a 5×5 matrix of zeros, and $\bar{\Sigma}_g$ satisfies

$$\text{vec}\left(\bar{\Sigma}_g\right) = \left(I_{100} - \left(\bar{\Phi}_g \otimes \bar{\Phi}_g\right)\right)^{-1} \text{vec}\left(\bar{\Sigma}_\eta\right), \qquad (2.36)$$

where

$$\bar{\Phi}_g = \begin{bmatrix} \Phi_{g1} & \Phi_{g2} \\ I_5 & 0_5 \end{bmatrix} \quad \text{and} \quad \bar{\Sigma}_\eta = \begin{bmatrix} \Sigma_\eta & 0_5 \\ 0_5 & 0_5 \end{bmatrix}.$$

Here, vec($\cdot$) denotes the vectorization operator and $\otimes$ denotes the Kronecker product. Then, we have that

$$\beta^{(n)} = \left(\bar{\Sigma}_{g,11}\right)^{-1} [I_5 \ 0_5] \bar{\Sigma}_g \left(\Xi_2 [I_5 \ 0_5] - \Xi_1 \bar{\Phi}_g^{12}\right)' L_4', \qquad (2.37)$$

where Ξ_1 is the 4×5 matrix obtained from removing the last row of I_5 and Ξ_2 is the 4×5 matrix obtained from removing the first row of I_5.

To derive the population R^2, we first need to define

$$C_{g,12} := \mathbb{C}(g_{t+12}, g_t) = [I_5 \ 0_5] \bar{\Phi}_g^{12} \bar{\Sigma}_g [I_5 \ 0_5]'. \qquad (2.38)$$

---

[13] www.federalreserve.gov/data/nominal-yield-curve.htm.
[14] www.openicpsr.org/openicpsr/project/116041/version/V1/view.

Then, we have that

$$R_n^2 = \frac{\beta^{(n)\prime}\Sigma_{g,11}\beta^{(n)}}{\mathbb{V}\left(rx_{t+12}^{(n,12)}\right)}, \quad (2.39)$$

where

$$\mathbb{V}\left(rx_{t+12}^{(n,12)}\right) = e_n' L_4 \left[\Xi_2 \Sigma_{g,11} \Xi_2' + \Xi_1 \Sigma_{g,11} \Xi_1' \right.$$
$$\left. - \Xi_1 C_{g,12} \Xi_2' - \Xi_2 C_{g,12}' \Xi_1'\right] L_4' e_n,$$

and e_n is a 4×1 vector with a one corresponding to maturity n and zero elsewhere.

2.5.3 Additional Details on Implementation

To implement the bootstrap in empirical applications or our simulations, we use the following steps.

1. Let $\widehat{\beta}_{(s)}^{(n)}$ be the OLS estimator of equation (2.33) in the sth simulation. Calculate $\widehat{\Omega}_{(s)}$, the Newey-West HAC estimator with h lags.
2. For inference on the ith element of $\beta^{(n)}$, let us first define e_i as the 5×1 vector with a one in the ith position and zeros elsewhere. Then, we can write the null hypothesis as $\mathbb{H}_0 : e_i' \beta^{(n)} = e_i' \beta_0^{(n)}$ with the corresponding t-statistic

$$\widehat{t}_{i(s)} = \frac{e_i'\left(\widehat{\beta}_{(s)}^{(n)} - \beta_0^{(n)}\right)}{\text{SE}_i\left(\widehat{\beta}_{(s)}^{(n)}\right)}, \quad (2.40)$$

where $\text{SE}_i\left(\widehat{\beta}_{(s)}^{(n)}\right) = \sqrt{e_i'\widehat{\Omega}_{(s)} e_i}$.

3. Let $\widehat{\beta}_{(s),b}^{(n)*}$ be the OLS estimator of equation (2.33) in the bth bootstrap sample for the sth simulation. Calculate $\widehat{\Omega}_{(s),b}^*$, the Newey-West HAC estimator with h lags and define

$$\widehat{t}_{i(s),b}^* = \frac{e_i'\left(\widehat{\beta}_{(s),b}^{(n)*} - \widehat{\beta}_{(s)}^{(n)}\right)}{\text{SE}_i\left(\widehat{\beta}_{(s),b}^{(n)*}\right)}, \quad (2.41)$$

where $\text{SE}_i\left(\widehat{\beta}_{(s),b}^{(n)*}\right) = \sqrt{e_i'\widehat{\Omega}_{(s),b}^* e_i}$.

4. Form p-values for the symmetric percentile-t method as

$$\widehat{p}_{i(s)}^* = \frac{1}{B}\sum_{b=1}^{B} \mathbb{1}\left\{|\widehat{t}_{i(s),b}^*| > |\widehat{t}_{i(s)}|\right\}, \quad (2.42)$$

where $\mathbb{1}\{\cdot\}$ denotes the indicator function and B is the total number of bootstrap replications.

5. For a test of nominal size α (e.g., $\alpha = 0.1$ or 10%), we reject the null hypothesis if $\widehat{p}^*_{i(s)} < \alpha$. To obtain empirical size across simulations, we calculate

$$\widehat{\alpha}(S) = \frac{1}{S}\sum_{s=1}^{S} \mathbb{1}\left\{\widehat{p}^*_{i(s)} < \alpha\right\}, \tag{2.43}$$

where S is the total number of simulations.

6. To calculate size-adjusted empirical power, construct for each simulation

$$\widetilde{t}^A_{i(s)} = \frac{e'_i\left(\widehat{\beta}^{(n)}_{(s)} - \beta^{(n)}_A\right)}{\operatorname{SE}_i\left(\widehat{\beta}^{(n)}_{(s)}\right)} \tag{2.44}$$

for the alternative hypothesis, $\mathbb{H}_A : e'_i\beta^{(n)} = e'_i\beta^{(n)}_A$. Next, calculate

$$\widehat{p}^{A*}_{i(s)} = \frac{1}{B}\sum_{b=1}^{B} \mathbb{1}\left\{|\widehat{t}^*_{i(s),b}| > |\widetilde{t}^A_{i(s)}|\right\}. \tag{2.45}$$

Finally, calculate size-adjusted empirical power as

$$\frac{1}{S}\sum_{s=1}^{S} \mathbb{1}\left\{\widehat{p}^{A*}_{i(s)} < \mathsf{q}(\widehat{p}^*_{i(1)},\ldots,\widehat{p}^*_{i(S)}; \alpha)\right\}, \tag{2.46}$$

where $\mathsf{q}(\widehat{p}^*_{i(1)},\ldots,\widehat{p}^*_{i(S)}; \alpha)$ is the αth quantile of the $\widehat{p}^*_{i(s)}$ across simulations.

3 Nominal and Real Yield Curves

A number of countries issue inflation-linked bonds in addition to the nominal bonds that we studied in the previous section. In the United States, these are informally referred to as TIPS, which stands for Treasury Inflation-Protected Securities. Unlike nominal Treasury bonds, which pay a fixed principal, TIPS have an uncertain principal payment that depends on the accumulated path of inflation over the life of the bond.[15] One of the main appeals of a security with properties like TIPS is that it elicits information about the real yield curve, that is, the term structure of real interest rates. The nominal and real curves are then linked by inflation and so their joint behavior allows market participants and policymakers to infer market views on the path of future prices. In this section, we show how to extend our bootstrap procedure to jointly bootstrap nominal and real yield curves in a fashion that preserves their internal consistency.

---

[15] For more information about the TIPS market see, for example, Campbell and Shiller (1996), Sack and Elsasser (2004), Dudley, Roush, and Ezer (2009), Fleming and Krishnan (2012), Fleckenstein, Longstaff, and Lustig (2014), Rebonato (2018), and Andreasen, Christensen, and Riddell (2021).

3.1 Notation and Properties of the Data

Let us denote the price of a zero-coupon TIPS bond at time t and maturity n as $P_t^{R(n)}$. Throughout this section we differentiate real bond characteristics using the superscript "R" while their nominal counterparts remain unchanged from the notation introduced in Section 2. This zero-coupon TIPS bond makes a single principal payment n years hence of Q_{t+n}/Q_t, where Q_t is the consumer price index at time t.[16] We denote the corresponding log price of this bond as $p_t^{R(n)}$ and define the log real yield as

$$y_t^{R(n)} := -\frac{1}{n} p_t^{R(n)}. \tag{3.1}$$

The n-maturity breakeven yield, $BEI_t^{y(n)}$, is defined as,

$$BEI_t^{y(n)} := y_t^{(n)} - y_t^{R(n)}. \tag{3.2}$$

This may also be referred to as n-maturity breakeven inflation or inflation compensation.

Real forward rates can be defined in a similar way to nominal bonds, namely,

$$f_t^{R(n,h)} := p_t^{R(n-h)} - p_t^{R(n)}, \qquad f_t^{R(n)} =: f_t^{R(n,1)}. \tag{3.3}$$

Furthermore, the h-period breakeven forward, $(n-h)$ periods ahead, $BEI_t^{f(n,h)}$, can then be defined as

$$BEI_t^{f(n,h)} := f_t^{(n,h)} - f_t^{R(n,h)}, \qquad BEI_t^{f(n)} =: BEI_t^{f(n,1)}. \tag{3.4}$$

As an example, with monthly real and nominal yield curve data, the one-year breakeven forward, nine years ahead would be $BEI_t^{f(120,12)}$.

Finally, the h-period holding return is

$$r_t^{R(n,h)} := p_t^{R(n-h)} - p_{t-h}^{R(n)}, \qquad r_t^{R(n)} =: r_t^{R(n,1)}. \tag{3.5}$$

The h-period holding return in excess of the (nominal) risk-free rate is

$$rx_t^{R(n,h)} := r_t^{R(n,h)} + p_{t-h}^{(h)}, \qquad rx_t^{R(n)} =: rx_t^{R(n,1)}. \tag{3.6}$$

We will also make use of the following alternative measure of returns,

$$rr_t^{R(n,h)} := r_t^{R(n,h)} + p_{t-h}^{R(h)}, \qquad rr_t^{R(n)} =: rr_t^{R(n,1)}, \tag{3.7}$$

which is the h-period holding return in excess of the h-period *real* rate. For the TIPS market, we cannot reliably calculate $rr_t^{R(n,h)}$ unless h is at least two years (see Gürkaynak, Sack, & Wright, 2010). However, this object will be used in some of the following theoretical derivations.

---

[16] In this section, we are abstracting from the CPI indexation lag in TIPS. Since our focus is on longer maturity nominal and real bonds, this simplification should not unduly affect the results.

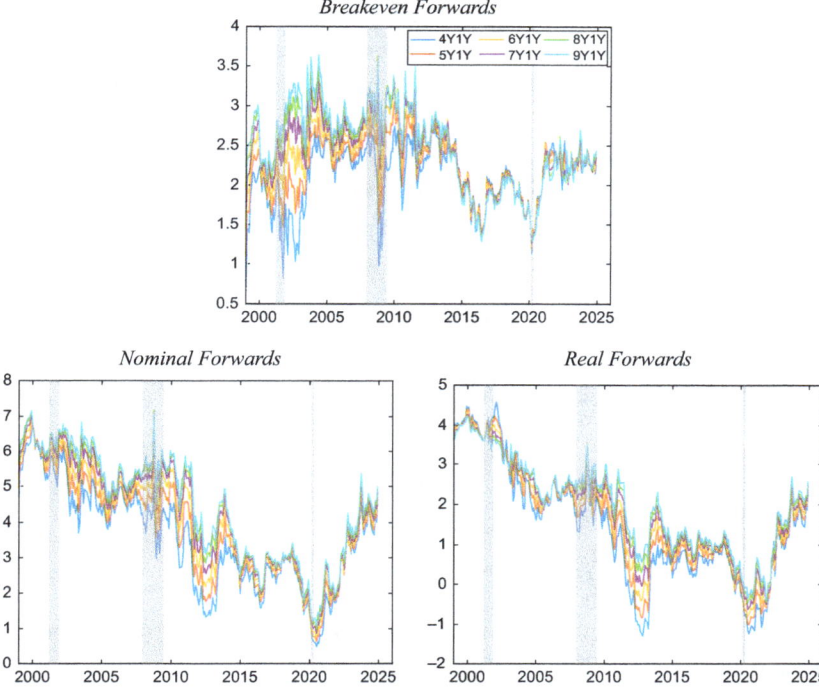

Figure 5 Treasury and TIPS Forward Rates. This figure presents the time series of one-year forward rates (four years to nine years ahead) from the breakeven, nominal, and real forward yield curves (in percent, annualized). The sample period is 1999m1–2024m12 using monthly data from Gürkaynak, Sack, and Wright (2007, 2010). Grey shaded areas denote NBER recessions.

The two curves are linked via breakeven inflation which can have differential behavior as compared to its two parent curves. Crump, Gospodinov, and Volker (2021) showed how the breakeven forward curve can behave in a markedly different way than either the nominal curve or the real curve. In particular, they highlight how the forward breakeven curve compressed strikingly in 2014. The top chart of Figure 5 shows the one-year forward breakeven rates starting four years into the future (4Y1Y) to nine years into the future (9Y1Y). Prior to 2014, there is a wide spread in the level of forward breakeven rates with a range averaging more than 70 basis points. Starting in 2014, and continuing through the end of our sample in 2024, the range declined sharply, averaging only 13 basis points. Importantly the compression of forward breakeven rates is not mirrored in the nominal and real forward curves themselves (bottom row of Figure 5). It is also important to note that the compression in the forward breakeven curve continued both in the 2014–2019 period, which featured a downward shift in the level of breakevens, and the post-COVID period where breakevens are around the bottom of their pre-2009 range. These empirical observations demonstrate clearly that it is insufficient to study the nominal and real yield curves separately.

We can also illustrate the important linkages between the two curves by decomposing yields into their expectations and risk premium components.[17] We can define the n-maturity nominal and real term premia as

$$TP_t^{(n)} := y_t^{(n)} - \frac{1}{n}\sum_{i=0}^{n-1} \mathbb{E}_t\left[y_{t+i}^{(1)}\right] \tag{3.8}$$

$$TP_t^{R(n)} := y_t^{R(n)} - \frac{1}{n}\sum_{i=0}^{n-1} \mathbb{E}_t\left[y_{t+i}^{R(1)}\right], \tag{3.9}$$

where $\mathbb{E}_t[\cdot] = \mathbb{E}[\cdot|\mathcal{F}_t]$ and $\mathcal{F}_t$ is the information set at time t. The inflation risk premium is the difference between these two term premia,

$$IRP_t^{(n)} = TP_t^{(n)} - TP_t^{R(n)}. \tag{3.10}$$

The inflation risk premium is an important object as it allows for extracting inflation expectations from breakeven rates since

$$BEI_t^{y(n)} = \frac{1}{n}\sum_{i=0}^{n-1} \mathbb{E}_t\left[\pi_{t+i+1}^{(1)}\right] + IRP_t^{(n)}, \tag{3.11}$$

where $\pi_t^{(1)} := \log\left(\frac{Q_{t+1}}{Q_t}\right)$ is the one-period inflation rate.

There are two approaches to infer the characteristics of the (latent) inflation risk premium. The first approach is to use parametric term structure models; for example, as in Abrahams et al. (2016), Gospodinov and Wei (2016), or D'Amico, Kim, and Wei (2018). The second approach is to perform predictive return regressions on an appropriately modified dependent variable; for example, as in Pflueger and Viceira (2016). Here, we introduce a novel perspective on the second approach, which we outline next.

Following Cochrane and Piazzesi (2008), we can link the term premium to the expected returns on nominal and real bonds via

$$TP_t^{(n)} = \frac{1}{n}\sum_{i=0}^{n-2} \mathbb{E}_t\left[rx_{t+1+i}^{(n-i)}\right], \tag{3.12}$$

---

[17] For simplicity, we ignore convexity effects and liquidity premia in our discussion. For more information on the former, see, for example, Rebonato (2018), and for more information on the latter see, for example, Abrahams et al. (2016), D'Amico, Kim, and Wei (2018), and Andreasen, Christensen, and Riddell (2021).

$$TP_t^{R(n)} = \frac{1}{n}\sum_{i=0}^{n-2} \mathbb{E}_t\left[rr_{t+1+i}^{R(n-i)}\right], \qquad (3.13)$$

which implies

$$IRP_t^{(n)} = \frac{1}{n}\sum_{i=0}^{n-2} \mathbb{E}_t\left[rx_{t+1+i}^{(n-i)} - rr_{t+1+i}^{R(n-i)}\right]. \qquad (3.14)$$

To study the behavior of $TP_t^{R(n)}$ and $IRP_t^{(n)}$, we can exploit the following identities:

$$\mathbb{E}_t\left[rr_{t+1+i}^{R(n-i)}\right] = \mathbb{E}_t\left[r_{t+1+i}^{R(n-i)} - y_{t+i}^{R(1)}\right] = \mathbb{E}_t\left[rx_{t+1+i}^{R(n-i)} + \pi_{t+1+i}^{(1)}\right], \qquad (3.15)$$

and

$$\begin{aligned}\mathbb{E}_t\left[rx_{t+1+i}^{(n-i)} - rr_{t+1+i}^{R(n-i)}\right] &= \mathbb{E}_t\left[r_{t+1+i}^{(n-i)} - y_{t+i}^{(1)} - r_{t+1+i}^{R(n-i)} + y_{t+i}^{R(1)}\right] \\ &= \mathbb{E}_t\left[r_{t+1+i}^{(n-i)} - r_{t+1+i}^{R(n-i)} - \pi_{t+1+i}^{(1)}\right].\end{aligned} \qquad (3.16)$$

To obtain these equivalences, we have utilized the law of iterated expectations and the Fisher equation,

$$y_t^{R(1)} = y_t^{(1)} - \mathbb{E}_t\left[\pi_{t+1}^{(1)}\right]. \qquad (3.17)$$

An important advantage of the identities given by equations (3.15) and (3.16) is that we can learn about the drivers of the real risk premium and the inflation risk premium, respectively, without observing a short-maturity real yield. Instead, we can rely on price inflation which is directly observable (see equations (3.23) and (3.24)). An alternative approach would be to construct a proxy for a short-maturity real yield (e.g., Campbell & Shiller, 1996; Pflueger & Viceira, 2016). This has the drawback that if the proxy is a poor approximation to the actual real yield, this may compromise the empirical results.

3.2 A Nonparametric Joint Bootstrap

Unfortunately, we cannot bootstrap the real yield curve in exactly the same way as the nominal yield curve because reliable short-maturity TIPS yields are not generally available. We follow the convention in Gürkaynak, Sack, and Wright (2010), who utilize real yields only starting at the two-year maturity.

Before presenting the joint bootstrap procedure we will start by discussing just the real yield curve. Suppose we observe the monthly prices of zero-coupon TIPS with maturities ranging from two to ten years, $\left(p_t^{R(24)}, p_t^{R(36)}, \ldots, p_t^{R(120)}\right)$. Following the steps from Section 2 given by equations (2.18) and (2.19), we can construct

$$z_{1,t}^R = 100 \cdot f_t^{R(120,12)}$$
$$z_{2,t}^R = 100 \cdot \left(f_t^{R(108,12)} - f_{t-1}^{R(120,12)}\right)$$
$$z_{3,t}^R = 100 \cdot \left(f_t^{R(96,12)} - f_{t-1}^{R(108,12)}\right)$$
$$\vdots$$
$$z_{8,t}^R = 100 \cdot \left(f_t^{R(36,12)} - f_{t-1}^{R(48,12)}\right). \quad (3.18)$$

Here we multiply by a factor of 100 when forming $z_{1,t}^R$ through $z_{10,t}^R$ so that they are expressed as percent. Throughout the rest of the section we will work with all series in annualized percentage terms. We did not need to be explicit about this distinction in Section 2 as the bootstrap algorithm in the nominal case is invariant to scaling so long as it is consistently applied. In contrast, the bootstrap algorithm we introduce shortly would need to be modified appropriately if forwards, returns and inflation were expressed in other terms.

There is one vital difference with real yields, as shown by this series of equations (3.18), relative to their nominal counterpart. If we observe an initial set of prices at time 1 and all $(z_{1,t}^R, \ldots, z_{8,t}^R)$, we *cannot* obtain the time series of real yields $(y_t^{R(24)}, \ldots, y_t^{R(120)})$. This is because we do not have an identifying condition that maps $z_{8,t}^R$ to the price of a single zero-coupon TIPS, that is, we can only obtain $f_t^{R(36,12)}$, which is $p_t^{R(24)} - p_t^{R(36)}$, but not $p_t^{R(24)}$ or $p_t^{R(36)}$ separately. Instead, we need to endow the bootstrap procedure with additional information. In particular, we will add $w_{1,t} = \pi_t^{yoy}$ and $w_{2,t} = BEI_t^{y(24)} - \pi_t^{yoy}$, where π_t^{yoy} is year-over-year inflation. Then, we can back out $y_t^{R(24)}$, and hence $p_t^{R(24)}$, using the equality, $y_t^{R(24)} = y_t^{(24)} - w_{1,t} - w_{2,t}$.

We can now lay out the full bootstrap approach. As in Section 2, we assume we also observe nominal bond prices $\left(p_t^{(12)}, \ldots, p_t^{(120)}\right)$. Define the $(T-1) \times 20$ matrix $Z^{N,R}$ which has tth row equal to

$$\left(\tilde{z}_{1,t+1}, z_{2,t+1}, \ldots, z_{10,t+1}, \tilde{z}_{1,t+1}^R, z_{2,t+1}^R, \ldots, z_{8,t+1}^R, \tilde{w}_{1,t+1}, \tilde{w}_{2,t+1}\right),$$

where, again, all series are expressed in annualized percentage terms. We obtain $(\tilde{z}_{1,t+1}, \tilde{z}_{1,t+1}^R, \tilde{w}_{1,t+1}, \tilde{w}_{2,t+1})$ from the following VAR(1) used for pre-whitening

$$\begin{pmatrix} f_{t+1}^{(120,12)} \\ f_{t+1}^{R(120,12)} \\ \pi_{t+1}^{yoy} \\ BEI_{t+1}^{y(24)} - \pi_{t+1}^{yoy} \end{pmatrix} = \hat{\mu} + \hat{\Phi} \begin{pmatrix} f_t^{(120,12)} \\ f_t^{R(120,12)} \\ \pi_t^{yoy} \\ BEI_t^{y(24)} - \pi_t^{yoy} \end{pmatrix} + \begin{pmatrix} \tilde{z}_{1,t+1} \\ \tilde{z}_{1,t+1}^R \\ \tilde{w}_{1,t+1}, \\ \tilde{w}_{2,t+1} \end{pmatrix}, \quad (3.19)$$

where $\hat{\mu}$ and $\hat{\Phi}$ may be obtained from OLS estimation. As in Section 2, all initial conditions in recursive steps use the first observation of the data.

The bootstrap algorithm then consists of the following steps:

Step 1: Block bootstrap $Z^{N,R}$ to obtain $Z^{N,R*}$.

Step 2: Use equation (3.19) to obtain the bootstrapped time series of
$$\left(f_t^{(120,12)*}, f_t^{R(120,12)*}, \pi_t^{yoy*}, BEI_t^{y(24)*} - \pi_t^{yoy*}\right), \qquad t = 1, \ldots, T.$$

Step 3: Follow Step 3 of the nominal bootstrap (see Section 2.2) to obtain the time series of nominal bond prices
$$\left(p_t^{(12)*}, p_t^{(24)*} \ldots, p_t^{(120)*}\right), \qquad t = 1, \ldots, T,$$
and corresponding bond yields,
$$\left(y_t^{(12)*}, y_t^{(24)*} \ldots, y_t^{(120)*}\right), \qquad t = 1, \ldots, T.$$

Step 4: Construct the time series of $y_t^{R(24)*}$ as $y_t^{R(24)*} = y_t^{(24)*} - BEI_t^{y(24)*}$ for $t = 1, \ldots, T$.

Step 5: Using the recursive relationship in equation (3.18), obtain the time series of
$$\left(f_t^{R(36,12)*}, f_t^{R(48,12)*} \ldots, f_t^{R(120,12)*}\right), \qquad t = 1, \ldots, T.$$

Step 6: Obtain the time series of $y_t^{R(n)*}$ for $n \in \{36, \ldots, 120\}$ using the recursive equation
$$y_t^{R(n)*} = \frac{12}{n}\left(f_t^{R(n,12)*} + \left(\frac{n-12}{12}\right) y_t^{R(n-12)*}\right).$$

Step 7: Repeat Steps 1–6 to obtain B bootstrap samples.

Following Steps 1–6 produces a single *joint* bootstrap sample of the nominal yield curve, the real yield curve, and the year-over-year inflation rate. As discussed in Section 2 one may also want to jointly resample the nominal and real yield curves with an external set of variables. To do so we need only add these external variables to the VAR(1) in equation (3.19) and then modify Step 2 accordingly.

3.3 Simulation Evidence

We design a simulation study to evaluate the finite-sample properties of our new joint bootstrap. In particular, we assume that the joint nominal and real yield curves follow a six-dimensional factor structure featuring three nominal factors, two breakeven factors, and year-over-year inflation. In particular, we assume that

$$F_t = \mathbf{a}^f + \mathbf{B}^f g_t + \xi_t, \qquad (3.20)$$

where

$$g_t = \mu_g + \Phi_g g_{t-1} + \eta_t^g, \tag{3.21}$$

and ξ_t and η_t^g are random vectors which are mutually independent multivariate Gaussian white noise. Here,

$$F_t = \left(y_t^{(12)}, f_t^{(24,12)}, \ldots, f_t^{(120,12)}, y_t^{R(24)}, f_t^{R(36,12)}, \ldots, f_t^{R(120,12)}\right)',$$

and $g_t = (y_t^{(12)}, f_t^{(60,12)}, f_t^{(120,12)}, BEI_t^{f(36,12)}, BEI_t^{f(120,12)}, \pi_t^{yoy})'$.

We place restrictions on the parameters of the data-generating process. Because we use forward rates as factors, the variance-covariance matrix of ξ_t has a reduced-rank structure that we impose in the calibration. We also place restrictions on $\mathbf{a}^f$, $\mathbf{B}^f$ and Φ_g. First, we restrict the last element of $\mathbf{a}^f$ and the last row of $\mathbf{B}^f$ to be zero. Second, we restrict the first five entries of the last column of Φ_g to be zero so that past nominal and real yield curve factors may forecast future inflation but the converse is not true. Combining these two restrictions implies that inflation is not a priced factor and does not predict future nominal or real yields. We choose these restrictions for the simulation design as it makes accurate inference more challenging and, thus, a better test of our bootstrap. We calibrate all necessary parameters using data from Gürkaynak, Sack, and Wright (2007, 2010) over the sample 1999m1–2024m12. For reference, Φ_g is calibrated as a highly persistent vector-valued process with a minimum (absolute) eigenvalue of 0.66 and a maximum eigenvalue of 0.985.

We assess the performance of our bootstrap procedure in the following three types of predictive regressions:

$$rx_{t+12}^{(n,12)} = \alpha^{(n)} + \beta^{(n)'} g_t + \varepsilon_{t+12}^{(n,12)}, \tag{3.22}$$

$$rx_{t+12}^{R(n,12)} + \pi_{t+12}^{yoy} = \alpha^{R(n)} + \beta^{R(n)'} g_t + \varepsilon_{t+12}^{R(n,12)}, \tag{3.23}$$

and

$$r_{t+12}^{(n,12)} - r_{t+12}^{R(n,12)} - \pi_{t+12}^{yoy} = \alpha^{IRP(n)} + \beta^{IRP(n)'} g_t + \varepsilon_{t+12}^{IRP(n,12)}. \tag{3.24}$$

One could also modify equation (3.23) using only $rx_{t+12}^{R(n,12)}$ to assess the predictability of excess returns from a TIPS investment. This may also be of interest and can be accommodated easily in our framework.

The true values of the regression parameters for equations (3.22)–(3.24) can be obtained analytically and are provided in Section 3.5.2 in the Appendix. We utilize the bootstrap introduced in Section 3.2 based on $B = 399$ replications with choice of block size:

$$M = (\max\{N_N, N_R\} \cdot T)^{2/5}. \tag{3.25}$$

Since both $N_R = 120$ and $N_N = 120$, we obtain $M = (120 \cdot T)^{2/5}$. All results are based on 5,000 simulations and a sample size of $T = 300$. We report empirical size using a nominal level of 10% and the associated (size-adjusted) power based on the test of the null hypothesis that the regression coefficient is zero. See Section 2.5.3 for full details on calculating empirical size and power across simulations.

As in Section 2, we compare our bootstrap to three different alternatives. The first one is an oracle bootstrap that uses the full parametric structure of the data-generating process, including knowledge of the true parameters. The only sampling uncertainty in this method arises from the randomness generated from the $B = 399$ simulated draws of ξ_t and η_t^g. As $B \to \infty$, the oracle procedure, centered at the true parameter value, obtains the exact finite-sample distribution of the t-statistic. Second, we use the conventional Newey and West (1987) variance estimator based on $h = 12$ lags (labeled "NW"). Finally, we also make comparisons to the inference procedure introduced in Lazarus et al. (2018) using the equal-weighted cosine (EWC) estimator of the long-run variance and a limiting-t distribution (labeled "LLSW-EWC").[18]

Table 2 presents the results for the predictive regression in equation (3.22) for selected maturities.[19] The left panel reports the empirical size for t-tests that the coefficient associated with g_{it} for $i \in \{1, \ldots, 6\}$ is equal to the true coefficient. The right panel reports size-adjusted (SA) power for the t-test that the coefficient associated with g_{it} is equal to zero. Since the last element of $\beta^{(n)}$ is zero, we only report SA power for the first five coefficients.[20] We can first observe that the CG bootstrap results in tests with empirical size near the nominal level of 10% across maturities and variables. There are some modest size distortions with slight over-rejections and under-rejections but, in general, the procedure controls size well. By contrast, test statistics that utilize HAC/HAR estimators (Newey-West and LLSW-EWC) suffer from severe size distortions likely resulting from the high cross-sectional and time-series dependence in the data.

In terms of power, the right panel of Table 2 shows that the size control exhibited by the (nonparametric) CG bootstrap does not come at the expense

---

[18] The MATLAB replication package also produces results for the LLSW-NW procedure, which are almost uniformly dominated by the LLSW-EWC alternative.

[19] Some maturities are omitted to conserve space. The qualitative conclusions discussed are unchanged for these omitted maturities. Results for all maturities are available in the companion MATLAB code.

[20] This is not the case for the last element of $\beta^{R(n)}$ or $\beta^{IRP(n)}$ which have nonzero values reflecting the marginal predictive power of past inflation for future inflation. Results for (size-adjusted) power for these coefficients are available in the MATLAB replication code.

Table 2 Nominal Bond Returns. This table presents empirical size and size-adjusted (SA) power for the predictive regression given by equation (3.22). The nominal level is 10% and the sample size is $T = 300$. Each column reports results for the t-test associated with the regressor g_{it}, $i \in \{1,\ldots,6\}$. Each row reports results for bond returns of the corresponding maturity. Based on 5,000 simulations and 399 bootstrap replications per simulation.

	CG Bootstrap										
	Size						SA Power				
	g_{1t}	g_{2t}	g_{3t}	g_{4t}	g_{5t}	g_{6t}	g_{1t}	g_{2t}	g_{3t}	g_{4t}	g_{5t}
2y	0.124	0.093	0.092	0.091	0.085	0.079	0.134	0.561	0.119	0.315	0.090
3y	0.115	0.111	0.101	0.089	0.080	0.077	0.245	0.674	0.165	0.272	0.097
5y	0.100	0.125	0.096	0.079	0.070	0.079	0.439	0.732	0.213	0.223	0.111
7y	0.097	0.129	0.089	0.074	0.071	0.088	0.511	0.717	0.198	0.180	0.124
10y	0.091	0.112	0.089	0.065	0.072	0.093	0.535	0.623	0.133	0.140	0.142
	Oracle Bootstrap										
	Size						SA Power				
2y	0.097	0.097	0.090	0.100	0.092	0.106	0.231	0.535	0.118	0.301	0.104
3y	0.097	0.095	0.094	0.102	0.094	0.102	0.356	0.664	0.161	0.262	0.100
5y	0.097	0.099	0.096	0.100	0.093	0.101	0.509	0.733	0.210	0.213	0.104
7y	0.104	0.099	0.096	0.100	0.094	0.100	0.561	0.714	0.188	0.178	0.116
10y	0.105	0.103	0.102	0.101	0.096	0.102	0.561	0.602	0.126	0.142	0.136
	Newey-West										
	Size						SA Power				
2y	0.375	0.263	0.247	0.244	0.210	0.305	0.228	0.536	0.115	0.306	0.099
3y	0.359	0.286	0.244	0.236	0.206	0.303	0.358	0.666	0.165	0.272	0.098
5y	0.342	0.303	0.249	0.231	0.206	0.308	0.512	0.735	0.201	0.211	0.108
7y	0.331	0.300	0.250	0.228	0.210	0.312	0.567	0.719	0.186	0.182	0.117
10y	0.328	0.292	0.263	0.227	0.211	0.326	0.560	0.613	0.130	0.148	0.136
	LLSW-EWC										
	Size						SA Power				
2y	0.304	0.204	0.186	0.198	0.159	0.242	0.235	0.527	0.118	0.297	0.096
3y	0.281	0.226	0.190	0.184	0.160	0.237	0.364	0.648	0.164	0.262	0.100
5y	0.265	0.247	0.193	0.180	0.162	0.242	0.502	0.725	0.202	0.203	0.106
7y	0.260	0.246	0.195	0.178	0.162	0.247	0.549	0.699	0.185	0.178	0.114
10y	0.259	0.227	0.204	0.175	0.163	0.256	0.541	0.598	0.129	0.135	0.133

of a material loss in power. We can draw this conclusion by comparing the SA power of the CG bootstrap to that of the infeasible oracle bootstrap.[21] The latter procedure exploits all knowledge of the true data-generating process and is, thus, the appropriate benchmark for comparison. Further, the SA power of the procedures that rely on asymptotic approximations to the distribution of the test statistic also have SA power comparable to that of the CG bootstrap. However, these power properties are for illustrative purposes only as these procedures cannot control type I errors. Finally, it is important to note that the finite-sample performance of the CG bootstrap mirrors that reported in Crump and Gospodinov (2025a) for the case of the nominal yield curve on its own; thus, despite the increased complexity of jointly bootstrapping two yield curves, there is no deterioration in performance.

Table 3 reports results for the predictive regression described by equation (3.23). The first maturity is now for the three-year TIPS bond, since the shortest-maturity yield that we observe is the two-year yield. The results are broadly in line with those of Table 2. Here, the CG bootstrap continues to control size, albeit with some mild over-rejections. Investigating further, we find that the OLS estimator for these coefficients exhibits meaningful finite-sample biases that affect the bootstrap procedure. The likely source of this bias is the large number of predictors, the high persistence of the underlying series, and the correlated nature of the predictors. These elements combine to forge a challenging inference environment. As in Table 2, approaches relying on HAC/HAR standard errors lead to more severe over-rejections.

The CG bootstrap continues to have size-adjusted power comparable to that of the other three procedures, including the infeasible oracle method. The power is largest for the first two nominal factors, reflecting the relatively large magnitude of the associated $\beta^{(n)}$ coefficients.

Table 4 presents results for the predictive regression given by equation (3.24). The results in this table are broadly similar to those of Tables 2 and 3. In predictive regressions assessing the behavior of the IRP, we observe that the CG bootstrap, again, controls size well and has power properties comparable to those of the alternative procedures we consider. Given that the predictive regressions described in equations (3.23) and (3.24) are new to the literature, it is encouraging that our bootstrap has reliable finite-sample performance to justify its use in empirical settings.

---

[21] Footnote 11 in Section 2 provides details on interpreting comparisons to the power of the oracle procedure.

Table 3 Real Bond Returns. This table presents empirical size and size-adjusted (SA) power for the predictive regression given by equation (3.23). The nominal level is 10% and the sample size is $T = 300$. Each column reports results for the t-test associated with the regressor g_{it}, $i \in \{1,\ldots,6\}$. Each row reports results for bond returns of the corresponding maturity. Based on 5,000 simulations and 399 bootstrap replications per simulation.

	CG Bootstrap										
	Size						SA Power				
	g_{1t}	g_{2t}	g_{3t}	g_{4t}	g_{5t}	g_{6t}	g_{1t}	g_{2t}	g_{3t}	g_{4t}	g_{5t}
3y	0.067	0.100	0.087	0.063	0.080	0.156	0.341	0.229	0.091	0.982	0.173
5y	0.063	0.152	0.100	0.059	0.078	0.108	0.545	0.517	0.172	0.989	0.111
7y	0.069	0.157	0.095	0.056	0.074	0.089	0.571	0.523	0.146	0.964	0.149
10y	0.074	0.146	0.086	0.057	0.076	0.079	0.586	0.432	0.097	0.872	0.285

	Oracle Bootstrap										
	Size						SA Power				
	g_{1t}	g_{2t}	g_{3t}	g_{4t}	g_{5t}	g_{6t}	g_{1t}	g_{2t}	g_{3t}	g_{4t}	g_{5t}
3y	0.099	0.104	0.101	0.097	0.098	0.098	0.409	0.224	0.101	0.988	0.185
5y	0.099	0.102	0.105	0.098	0.094	0.098	0.587	0.557	0.160	0.994	0.113
7y	0.103	0.107	0.107	0.098	0.094	0.099	0.602	0.542	0.135	0.972	0.150
10y	0.106	0.109	0.104	0.098	0.093	0.100	0.609	0.431	0.099	0.870	0.267

	Newey-West										
	Size						SA Power				
	g_{1t}	g_{2t}	g_{3t}	g_{4t}	g_{5t}	g_{6t}	g_{1t}	g_{2t}	g_{3t}	g_{4t}	g_{5t}
3y	0.268	0.232	0.220	0.195	0.182	0.318	0.413	0.227	0.099	0.989	0.188
5y	0.283	0.295	0.240	0.214	0.197	0.291	0.584	0.559	0.166	0.994	0.115
7y	0.303	0.312	0.242	0.212	0.209	0.291	0.608	0.546	0.137	0.972	0.150
10y	0.320	0.310	0.246	0.210	0.212	0.297	0.606	0.433	0.100	0.871	0.267

	LLSW-EWC										
	Size						SA Power				
	g_{1t}	g_{2t}	g_{3t}	g_{4t}	g_{5t}	g_{6t}	g_{1t}	g_{2t}	g_{3t}	g_{4t}	g_{5t}
3y	0.213	0.187	0.173	0.150	0.144	0.263	0.404	0.225	0.097	0.986	0.189
5y	0.213	0.240	0.189	0.158	0.155	0.232	0.567	0.544	0.164	0.993	0.116
7y	0.236	0.258	0.187	0.160	0.160	0.226	0.594	0.538	0.138	0.968	0.144
10y	0.248	0.255	0.192	0.162	0.165	0.234	0.601	0.430	0.102	0.862	0.266

Table 4 Relative Nominal/Real Bond Returns. This table presents empirical size and size-adjusted (SA) power for the predictive regression given by equation (3.24). The nominal level is 10% and the sample size is $T = 300$. Each column reports results for the t-test associated with the regressor g_{it}, $i \in \{1,\ldots,6\}$. Each row reports results for bond returns of the corresponding maturity. Based on 5,000 simulations and 399 bootstrap replications per simulation.

	CG Bootstrap										
	Size						SA Power				
	g_{1t}	g_{2t}	g_{3t}	g_{4t}	g_{5t}	g_{6t}	g_{1t}	g_{2t}	g_{3t}	g_{4t}	g_{5t}
3y	0.025	0.079	0.081	0.056	0.079	0.129	0.080	0.249	0.148	0.777	0.159
5y	0.051	0.075	0.078	0.066	0.076	0.106	0.059	0.214	0.112	0.912	0.147
7y	0.065	0.076	0.075	0.074	0.076	0.101	0.055	0.227	0.124	0.915	0.304
10y	0.068	0.079	0.079	0.076	0.082	0.103	0.059	0.249	0.170	0.850	0.665
	Oracle Bootstrap										
	Size						SA Power				
3y	0.096	0.099	0.099	0.098	0.100	0.103	0.093	0.262	0.161	0.737	0.162
5y	0.095	0.097	0.101	0.099	0.096	0.104	0.103	0.231	0.112	0.913	0.150
7y	0.096	0.098	0.099	0.102	0.095	0.103	0.110	0.239	0.125	0.915	0.269
10y	0.100	0.100	0.099	0.104	0.097	0.099	0.110	0.271	0.174	0.850	0.671
	Newey-West										
	Size						SA Power				
3y	0.304	0.244	0.226	0.218	0.195	0.316	0.094	0.263	0.164	0.745	0.165
5y	0.322	0.243	0.234	0.246	0.206	0.310	0.102	0.231	0.114	0.916	0.147
7y	0.325	0.246	0.239	0.259	0.204	0.316	0.107	0.244	0.121	0.920	0.270
10y	0.320	0.248	0.249	0.253	0.206	0.320	0.108	0.274	0.173	0.853	0.680
	LLSW-EWC										
	Size						SA Power				
3y	0.239	0.187	0.175	0.173	0.154	0.256	0.097	0.260	0.159	0.729	0.165
5y	0.254	0.188	0.185	0.196	0.157	0.252	0.098	0.231	0.112	0.904	0.146
7y	0.253	0.185	0.187	0.205	0.163	0.253	0.102	0.242	0.125	0.905	0.272
10y	0.251	0.192	0.194	0.206	0.164	0.260	0.107	0.270	0.173	0.840	0.667

3.4 Empirical Application

Given the excellent finite-sample properties of the CG bootstrap in simulations, we can use this method to investigate the drivers of risk premia in the U.S. Treasury and TIPS markets. In this empirical application, we use monthly data over the sample period 1999m1–2024m12 (see Section 3.5.1 in the Appendix for a description of the data). We construct all necessary yield-curve objects, such as returns or forwards, using the definitions introduced in Section 3.1. To jointly bootstrap the Treasury and TIPS yield curves, we follow the steps outlined in Section 3.2.

Figure 6 presents the time series for selected variables along with their bootstrapped counterparts for a single bootstrap draw. This figure shows that the bootstrap successfully mimics the dynamics of these three yield-curve objects. This is surprising because conventional bootstrap procedures generally have a hard time capturing the dynamics of highly persistent series such as bond yields. The intuition for why our bootstrap differs from conventional approaches is the use of the accounting identities that we rely on. Thus, even though we resample individual series, which, themselves, have little persistence, once we reassemble different yield-curve objects, the correct persistence and variability of the original data are restored. Furthermore, the nonparametric nature of our bootstrap ensures that it replicates the cross-sectional dependence properties and preserves any underlying factor structure of the data.

In our empirical exercise, we use a common set of predictors in the predictive regression equations (3.22)–(3.24). While it may be natural to assume that there are different drivers of risk premia across these different assets, we use a common set of predictors for simplicity and to allow direct comparisons across regression specifications. We choose as our predictors: (1) the one-year breakeven forward, four years ahead (4Y1Y breakeven forward); (2) the nominal forward slope (9Y1Y forward less the one-year yield); (3) the real forward slope (9Y1Y forward less the 2Y1Y forward); and (4) year-over-year CPI inflation. All results are based on $B = 1,999$ bootstrap replications. We compare our bootstrapped p-values to those obtained using the equal-weighted cosine (EWC) variance estimator of Lazarus et al. (2018) based on a Student's t limiting distribution.[22]

All tables report point estimates for the slope coefficient, the bootstrapped p-value, the p-value based on the EWC variance estimator and the regression R^2. We present regression results of bond returns at one-year maturities up to ten years, starting at two years for nominal bonds and three years otherwise.

---

[22] We use the EWC variance estimator rather than the conventional Newey and West (1987) estimator as it performed better in our simulation experiments.

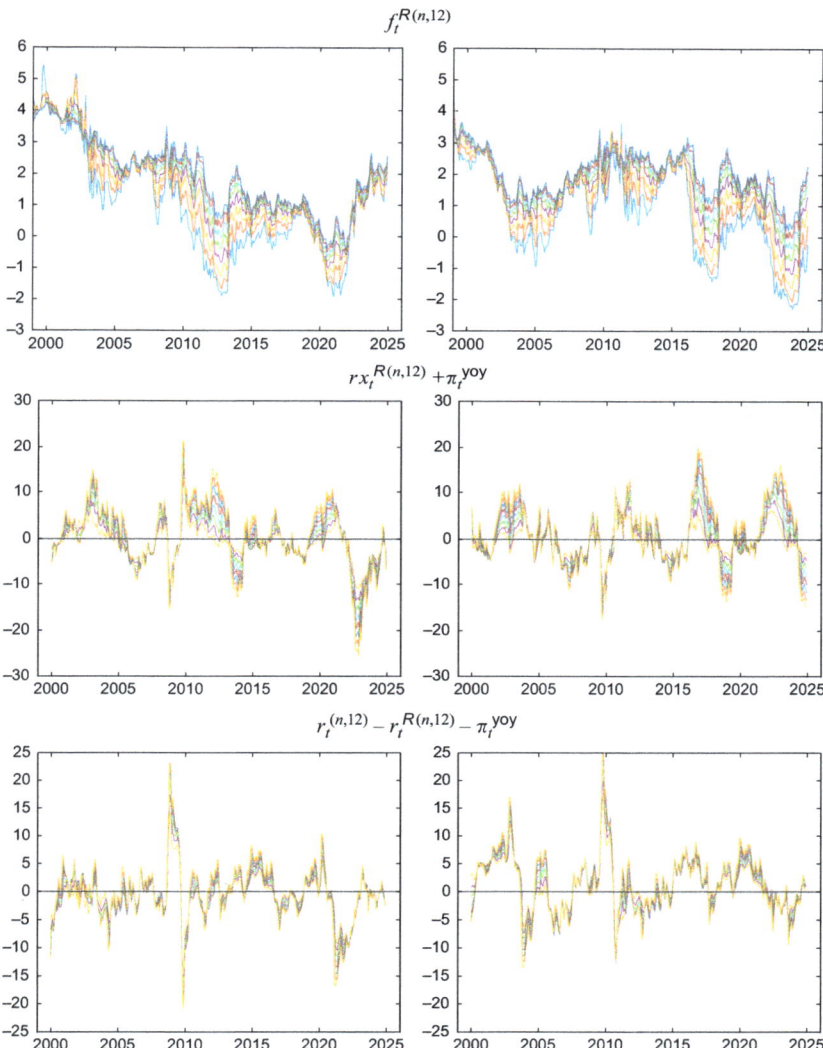

Figure 6 Realized Sample versus Bootstrapped Sample. The left column of this figure shows the time series of $f_t^{R(n,12)}$, $rx_t^{R(n,12)} + \pi_t^{yoy}$, and $r_t^{(n,12)} - r_t^{R(n,12)} - \pi_t^{yoy}$ for $n \in \{36, \ldots, 120\}$ (in percent, annualized). The sample period is 1999m1–2024m12 using monthly data from Gürkaynak, Sack, and Wright (2007, 2010). The right column of this figure shows the corresponding bootstrapped time series for these same objects.

The last row of each table presents the results for the cross-sectional average return across all available maturities.

Table 5 reports the regression results for nominal excess returns based on equation (3.22). The middle two panels present the results for the nominal

Table 5 Nominal Bond Returns. This table presents regression results from the predictive regression described by equation (3.22) for the four predictors described in the text. Results are provided for nominal bonds of maturity n ranging from two to 10 years and the cross-sectional average return (labeled "avg"). The table provides the OLS estimate, $\widehat{\beta}^{(n)}$, and the regression R^2, along with p-values for the null hypothesis of a zero coefficient. Bootstrap p-values are based on the bootstrap procedure introduced in Section 3.2 using $B = 1{,}999$, while asymptotic p-values are based on the EWC variance estimator of Lazarus et al. (2018).

	4Y1Y BE			Nom. Slope			Real Slope			Inflation			
	$\widehat{\beta}^{(n)}$	Boot. p-val	Asy. p-val	$\widehat{\beta}^{(n)}$	Boot. p-val	Asy. p-val	$\widehat{\beta}^{(n)}$	Boot. p-val	Asy. p-val	$\widehat{\beta}^{(n)}$	Boot. p-val	Asy. p-val	R^2
2y	0.43	[0.50]	[0.20]	0.15	[0.45]	[0.10]	−0.67	[0.01]	[0.00]	−0.28	[0.50]	[0.06]	0.23
3y	1.28	[0.29]	[0.09]	0.38	[0.23]	[0.05]	−1.41	[0.01]	[0.00]	−0.52	[0.45]	[0.04]	0.25
4y	2.27	[0.16]	[0.04]	0.64	[0.11]	[0.03]	−2.07	[0.00]	[0.00]	−0.73	[0.43]	[0.03]	0.27
5y	3.28	[0.07]	[0.02]	0.90	[0.05]	[0.02]	−2.65	[0.00]	[0.00]	−0.90	[0.44]	[0.03]	0.28
6y	4.23	[0.03]	[0.01]	1.16	[0.02]	[0.01]	−3.12	[0.00]	[0.00]	−1.05	[0.45]	[0.03]	0.29
7y	5.14	[0.01]	[0.00]	1.41	[0.01]	[0.01]	−3.51	[0.00]	[0.00]	−1.19	[0.46]	[0.03]	0.30
8y	5.99	[0.00]	[0.00]	1.64	[0.01]	[0.01]	−3.83	[0.00]	[0.00]	−1.32	[0.47]	[0.03]	0.30
9y	6.79	[0.00]	[0.00]	1.85	[0.00]	[0.01]	−4.10	[0.00]	[0.00]	−1.46	[0.48]	[0.03]	0.31
10y	7.56	[0.00]	[0.00]	2.04	[0.00]	[0.01]	−4.33	[0.00]	[0.00]	−1.60	[0.48]	[0.03]	0.31
avg.	4.11	[0.02]	[0.01]	1.13	[0.02]	[0.01]	−2.85	[0.00]	[0.00]	−1.01	[0.47]	[0.03]	0.30

and real forward slopes. The predictive power of the nominal slope has been widely documented and the bootstrapped *p*-values confirm this result, especially for excess returns of medium- to long-maturity bonds. Interestingly, the real slope also has strong predictive power for future nominal excess returns uniformly across the maturity spectrum. For the two spreads, the magnitude of the coefficient increases with maturity and both are highly significant predictors of average bond returns. Using asymptotic *p*-values for these predictors would lead to broadly similar conclusions. One exception is that the asymptotic *p*-values would suggest that the nominal slope also predicts excess returns on nominal short-maturity bonds, whereas the bootstrapped *p*-values exceed conventional levels of significance. A similar pattern emerges for the 4Y1Y breakeven forward where the two *p*-values are incongruent at shorter maturities but align for longer maturities.

The biggest difference in conclusions between bootstrap-based inference and conventional inference arises for the regression coefficients associated with inflation. Whereas the bootstrap *p*-values all exceed 0.43, the alternative *p*-values are below 0.05 for all but one maturity. We attribute this discrepancy to the fact that inflation is persistent and our bootstrap procedure jointly resamples inflation along with yields. This internalizes the co-movement between nominal yields, real yields, and realized inflation in each bootstrapped sample which is absent in conventional approaches. This result suggests that information about near-term developments in inflation is already incorporated in the yield-based predictors. Note that Cieslak and Povala (2015) and Crump and Gospodinov (2025a), using a much longer sample period, have shown that the low-frequency behavior of inflation is distinct from the information in yield-based predictors.

Table 6 presents the corresponding results for the predictive regression of equation (3.23).[23] We can first observe, based on the bootstrap *p*-values, that the nominal slope is the primary driver of variation in real risk premia in contrast to the results for nominal risk premia in Table 5. Furthermore, it is noteworthy that, despite broadly similar variability between these nominal and real returns, the regression R^2s are much higher in Table 6. In these regressions, the largest discrepancy between inference based on our bootstrap versus conventional standard errors is for the real slope and inflation. Using asymptotic *p*-values, one would conclude that both of these variables are strongly significant predictors of future returns whereas the bootstrapped *p*-values are, at best, only marginally significant at conventional levels for a few maturities.

---

[23] Existing studies have investigated real return predictability using alternative dependent variables and regression specifications (Pflueger & Viceira, 2016; Rebonato, 2024).

Table 6 Real Bond Returns. This table presents regression results from the predictive regression described by equation (3.23) for the four predictors described in the text. Results are provided for real bonds of maturity n ranging from three to 10 years and the cross-sectional average return (labeled "avg"). The table provides the OLS estimate, $\widehat{\beta}^{R(n)}$, and the regression R^2 along with p-values for the null hypothesis of a zero coefficient. Bootstrap p-values are based on the bootstrap procedure introduced in Section 3.2 using $B = 1{,}999$, while asymptotic p-values are based on the EWC variance estimator of Lazarus et al. (2018).

	4Y1Y BE			Nom. Slope			Real Slope			Inflation			
	$\widehat{\beta}^{R(n)}$	Boot. p-val	Asy. p-val	$\widehat{\beta}^{R(n)}$	Boot. p-val	Asy. p-val	$\widehat{\beta}^{R(n)}$	Boot. p-val	Asy. p-val	$\widehat{\beta}^{R(n)}$	Boot. p-val	Asy. p-val	R^2
3y	−2.11	[0.21]	[0.07]	0.34	[0.31]	[0.11]	−0.88	[0.33]	[0.09]	−0.70	[0.10]	[0.00]	0.38
4y	−2.11	[0.26]	[0.09]	0.61	[0.14]	[0.03]	−1.39	[0.14]	[0.03]	−0.89	[0.08]	[0.00]	0.44
5y	−2.05	[0.33]	[0.12]	0.83	[0.07]	[0.01]	−1.72	[0.10]	[0.02]	−1.04	[0.09]	[0.00]	0.45
6y	−1.96	[0.38]	[0.15]	1.02	[0.04]	[0.01]	−1.94	[0.11]	[0.02]	−1.16	[0.10]	[0.00]	0.44
7y	−1.86	[0.44]	[0.18]	1.17	[0.03]	[0.01]	−2.06	[0.13]	[0.03]	−1.27	[0.13]	[0.01]	0.43
8y	−1.77	[0.50]	[0.21]	1.29	[0.03]	[0.01]	−2.14	[0.16]	[0.04]	−1.37	[0.14]	[0.01]	0.41
9y	−1.68	[0.55]	[0.23]	1.40	[0.03]	[0.01]	−2.17	[0.18]	[0.04]	−1.46	[0.16]	[0.01]	0.39
10y	−1.60	[0.59]	[0.25]	1.49	[0.03]	[0.01]	−2.18	[0.20]	[0.05]	−1.56	[0.17]	[0.02]	0.38
avg.	−1.89	[0.41]	[0.16]	1.02	[0.05]	[0.01]	−1.81	[0.14]	[0.03]	−1.18	[0.12]	[0.01]	0.43

Finally, Table 7 reports results for the predictive regression of equation (3.24). Returns for bearing inflation risk are significantly predicted by the past 4Y1Y forward breakeven and the real slope, based on our bootstrap. This is consistent with the previous two tables where we saw that nominal returns were driven by the first three predictors (Table 5), whereas real returns were driven only by the nominal slope (Table 6). Since equation (3.24) may be written as the difference between equations (3.22) and (3.23), we would expect these two predictors to play a primary role. Taken in sum, this application highlights the utility of the joint bootstrap in helping to better understand the dynamics of nominal and real Treasury bonds.

3.5 Appendix to Section 3

3.5.1 Data Description

Throughout this section we rely on the zero-coupon yield curves for monthly maturities introduced in Gürkaynak, Sack, and Wright (2007)[24] and Gürkaynak, Sack, and Wright (2010)[25] which are available on the website of the Board of Governors of the Federal Reserve. Monthly data are constructed as the last available daily observation for each month. All series used follow the definitions introduced at the beginning of the section. To calculate inflation, we rely on the headline consumer price index, which is available, for example, on FRED with the mnemonic CPIAUCSL.[26]

3.5.2 Additional Details on Simulation Design

We construct the true coefficient values for equations (3.22)–(3.24) based on forward rates, yields, and returns in annualized percentage terms. For the predictive regressions of nominal excess returns described in equation (3.22), we have that

$$\begin{pmatrix} \beta^{(24)} \\ \vdots \\ \beta^{(120)} \end{pmatrix} = \mathsf{L}_9 \left(\Xi_2 \mathbf{B}^f - \Xi_1 \mathbf{B}^f \Phi_g^{12} \right), \tag{3.26}$$

where Ξ_1 is the 9×10 matrix obtained from removing the last row of I_{10}, and Ξ_2 is the 9×10 matrix obtained from removing the first row of I_{10}.

For the predictive regressions of real excess returns described in equation (3.23), we have that

---

[24] www.federalreserve.gov/data/nominal-yield-curve.htm.
[25] www.federalreserve.gov/data/tips-yield-curve-and-inflation-compensation.htm.
[26] https://fred.stlouisfed.org/series/CPIAUCSL.

Table 7 Relative Nominal/Real Bond Returns. This table presents regression results from the predictive regression described by equation (3.24) for the four predictors described in the text. Results are provided for bonds of maturity n ranging from three to 10 years and the cross-sectional average return (labeled "avg"). The table provides the OLS estimate, $\widehat{\beta}^{\mathrm{IRP}(n)}$, and the regression R^2 along with p-values for the null hypothesis of a zero coefficient. Bootstrap p-values are based on the bootstrap procedure introduced in Section 3.2 using $B = 1{,}999$, while asymptotic p-values are based on the EWC variance estimator of Lazarus et al. (2018).

	4Y1Y BE			Nom. Slope			Real Slope			Inflation			
	$\widehat{\beta}^{\mathrm{IRP}(n)}$	Boot. p-val	Asy. p-val	$\widehat{\beta}^{\mathrm{IRP}(n)}$	Boot. p-val	Asy. p-val	$\widehat{\beta}^{\mathrm{IRP}(n)}$	Boot. p-val	Asy. p-val	$\widehat{\beta}^{\mathrm{IRP}(n)}$	Boot. p-val	Asy. p-val	R^2
3y	3.38	[0.02]	[0.01]	0.04	[0.99]	[0.46]	−0.52	[0.43]	[0.24]	0.18	[0.65]	[0.29]	0.16
4y	4.38	[0.02]	[0.00]	0.02	[0.99]	[0.47]	−0.68	[0.32]	[0.20]	0.17	[0.71]	[0.32]	0.19
5y	5.32	[0.01]	[0.00]	0.07	[0.98]	[0.43]	−0.92	[0.22]	[0.14]	0.14	[0.76]	[0.36]	0.21
6y	6.19	[0.01]	[0.00]	0.15	[0.94]	[0.37]	−1.18	[0.13]	[0.10]	0.11	[0.83]	[0.40]	0.23
7y	7.00	[0.01]	[0.00]	0.24	[0.88]	[0.30]	−1.45	[0.08]	[0.06]	0.08	[0.89]	[0.43]	0.25
8y	7.75	[0.01]	[0.00]	0.35	[0.80]	[0.24]	−1.70	[0.05]	[0.04]	0.05	[0.94]	[0.46]	0.27
9y	8.47	[0.00]	[0.00]	0.45	[0.70]	[0.19]	−1.93	[0.04]	[0.03]	0.00	[0.99]	[0.50]	0.28
10y	9.16	[0.00]	[0.00]	0.54	[0.60]	[0.16]	−2.15	[0.03]	[0.02]	−0.04	[0.95]	[0.47]	0.30
avg.	6.46	[0.01]	[0.00]	0.23	[0.89]	[0.30]	−1.32	[0.10]	[0.07]	0.09	[0.87]	[0.42]	0.24

$$\begin{pmatrix} \beta^{R(36)} \\ \vdots \\ \beta^{R(120)} \end{pmatrix} = \Xi_4 \Xi_3 \Xi_6 \mathbf{B}^f - \Xi_7 \mathbf{B}^f - \Xi_5 \Xi_3 \Xi_6 \mathbf{B}^f \Phi_g^{12} + e_6' \Phi_g^{12}, \qquad (3.27)$$

where Ξ_6 is the 9×19 matrix $\Xi_6 = [0_{9\times 10} \; I_9]$ and Ξ_7 is the 8×19 matrix with all elements of the first column equal to one and zeros elsewhere. Further, $\Xi_4 = [0_{8\times 1} \; D_4]$ and $\Xi_5 = [D_5 \; 0_{8\times 1}]$, where D_4 is a diagonal matrix with diagonal entries $(3, 4, \ldots, 10)$ and D_5 is a diagonal matrix with diagonal entries $(2, 3, \ldots, 9)$. We define Ξ_3 to be a lower triangular matrix as follows: The first column of Ξ_3 has ith row equal to $2/(i + 1)$. For the jth column where $j = 2, \ldots, 9$, the (i, j) element of Ξ_3 equals $1/(i + 1)$ if $i \geq j$ and zero otherwise. Finally, e_6 is the 6×1 vector with last element equal to one and zeros elsewhere.

The true coefficients corresponding to equation (3.24) are then given by,

$$\begin{pmatrix} \beta^{IRP(36)} \\ \vdots \\ \beta^{IRP(120)} \end{pmatrix} = \begin{pmatrix} \beta^{(36)} \\ \vdots \\ \beta^{(120)} \end{pmatrix} - \begin{pmatrix} \beta^{R(36)} \\ \vdots \\ \beta^{R(120)} \end{pmatrix}. \qquad (3.28)$$

4 Equities

The predictability of stock returns has received enormous attention from market participants and academic researchers alike. This has spawned a vast empirical literature in search of systematic predictors of future stock returns.[27] It has also spawned a large econometrics literature on conducting inference in predictive regressions.[28] This literature highlights how this setting raises a number of statistical challenges that conventional inference approaches are ill-equipped to handle. Properly accounting for statistical uncertainty when investigating different investment strategies has been a key concern at least as far back as Cowles (1933).

In this section, we take a very different approach from that in the existing literature. We introduce a novel bootstrap procedure that utilizes the identities linking stock returns, dividends and prices and circumvents the need to impose a specific parametric process for the data. The appeal of a nonparametric bootstrap in this setting was first identified by Cowles (1933), who used an ingenious approach to resample the data without the benefits of

---

[27] See, for example, Campbell and Shiller (1988a,b), Fama and French (1988), Goetzmann and Jorion (1993), and for more recent contributions, the July 2008 issue of *Review of Financial Studies*, Rapach and Zhou (2013), and Goyal, Welch, and Zafirov (2024).

[28] See, for example, Hodrick (1992), Cavanagh, Elliott, and Stock (1995), Stambaugh (1999), Jansson and Moreira (2006), Campbell and Yogo (2006), Van Binsbergen and Koijen (2010), Wei and Wright (2013), and Kostakis, Magdalinos, and Stamatogiannis (2014).

modern computing. We build off this insight to quantify uncertainty without relying on strong assumptions on how the data were generated.

As was the case for the previous sections, we identify primitive objects that have appealing statistical properties for our bootstrap, and underpin important economic identities. In particular, we jointly block bootstrap price growth and dividend growth, as, together, they serve as fundamental drivers of the equity market as discussed in, for example, Cochrane (2007). Despite the fact that the time-series properties of these two series exhibit little serial correlation, persistent processes such as the dividend-price ratio, which are reconstructed from these primitive series via identities, retain their strong dependence properties in each bootstrapped sample. We also argue that predictive return regressions should, as a default, condition on the dividend-price ratio or the dividend yield, in addition to any other predictor (see also Ang & Bekaert, 2007).

4.1 Notation and Properties of the Data

Let P_t be the observed price of the stock (or portfolio of stocks) at time t and let D_t be the associated dividend. Then, we can define the gross return, $1 + R_t$, and the gross return excluding dividends (ex-dividends), $1 + R_t^{ex}$, as

$$1 + R_t := \frac{P_t + D_t}{P_{t-1}}, \quad 1 + R_t^{ex} = \frac{P_t}{P_{t-1}} =: PP_t. \tag{4.1}$$

These definitions imply that

$$(1 + R_t) - PP_t = \frac{D_t}{P_{t-1}} = DD_t \cdot DP_{t-1}, \tag{4.2}$$

where

$$DD_t := \frac{D_t}{D_{t-1}}, \quad DP_t := \frac{D_t}{P_t}. \tag{4.3}$$

In these equations, DD_t is the gross dividend growth at time t, and DP_t is the dividend-price ratio at time t.

The three ratios (PP_t, DD_t, and DP_t) will play a prominent role in our resampling procedure because returns can be written explicitly as

$$1 + R_t = PP_t + DD_t \cdot DP_{t-1}. \tag{4.4}$$

There are two key properties of equation (4.4). First, future returns are explicitly a function of the lagged dividend-price ratio. This follows by the definition of returns and so always holds in any dataset. Second, if we observe the lagged dividend-price ratio, DP_{t-1}, then the triplet, $(1 + R_t, PP_t, DD_t)$, is linearly related (i.e., if we know the value for two of the three, then we can always infer the value of the third). We exploit this property in our bootstrap procedure by resampling PP_t and DD_t so that we can recursively generate DP_t via

$$\frac{D_t}{P_t} = \left(\frac{D_{t-1}}{P_{t-1}}\right)\left(\frac{D_t}{D_{t-1}}\right)\left(\frac{P_t}{P_{t-1}}\right)^{-1} = DP_{t-1} \cdot DD_t \cdot PP_t^{-1}. \tag{4.5}$$

For practical convenience, we use the log-linear recursive equation

$$dp_t = dp_{t-1} + dd_t - pp_t = dp_0 + \sum_{j=1}^{t}(dd_j - pp_j) \tag{4.6}$$

with initial condition dp_0, where

$$dd_t = \log(DD_t), \quad pp_t = \log(PP_t), \quad dp_t = \log(DP_t). \tag{4.7}$$

Equity market data have a number of specific properties that differentiate them from those of other assets. To illustrate this, we use data from Welch and Goyal (2008), who directly provide R_t and PP_t for the S&P 500 stock index (see Section 4.5.1 in the Appendix for further details). The top row of Figure 7 shows the time series of gross returns and gross price growth. We can observe that both of these series have limited serial correlation with meaningful volatility and sharp downward spikes occurring in recessions. We should note that the differences between R_t and R_t^{ex} tend to be small in magnitude and so the two charts look very similar.

The charts in the bottom row of Figure 7 plot gross dividend growth and the dividend-price ratio. To obtain these series from the data, we utilize the identities

$$DP_t = \frac{1 + R_t}{PP_t} - 1 \tag{4.8}$$

and

$$DD_t = \frac{DP_t \cdot PP_t}{DP_{t-1}}. \tag{4.9}$$

The most noticeable feature in the bottom left chart is the pronounced seasonality in dividend growth, which produces systematic upward and downward spikes throughout the series, reflecting the timing of dividend payments. This seasonality is inherited by the dividend-price ratio, DP_t, as shown in the bottom right chart. To smooth the seasonality, researchers most frequently work with a modified dividend-price ratio series

$$DP_t^{(d)} = \frac{D_t + D_{t-1} + \cdots + D_{t-d+1}}{P_t}. \tag{4.10}$$

For annual data, we use $d = 1$ and obtain the standard dividend-price ratio, DP_t. However, for quarterly and monthly data we use $d = 4$ and $d = 12$, respectively,

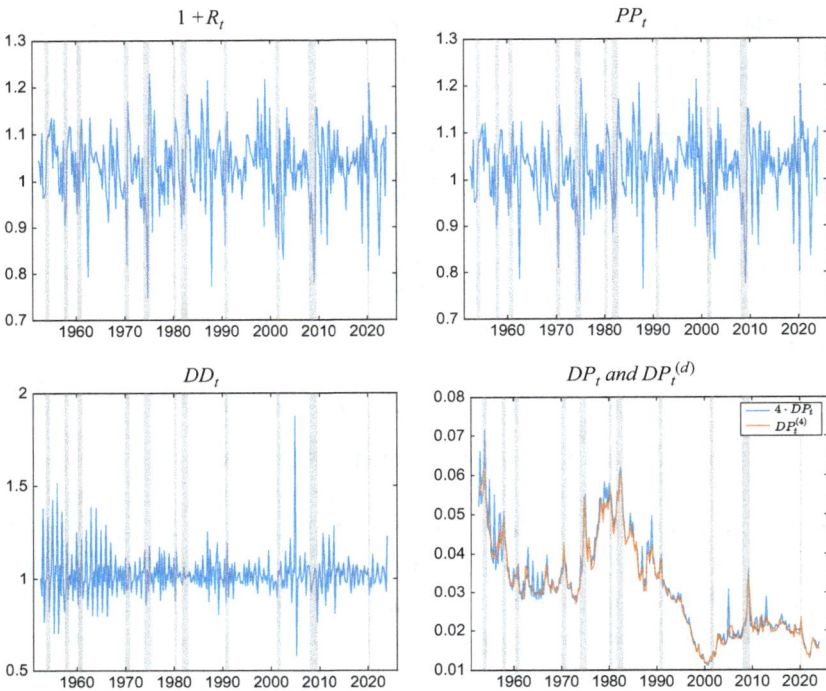

Figure 7 Main Components of Equity Returns. This figure presents the time series of gross returns, price growth, and dividend growth along with the dividend-price ratio. Note that we present the time series of $4 \cdot DP_t$ so it is on the same scale as $DP_t^{(4)}$. The sample period is 1952Q1–2023Q4 using data from Welch and Goyal (2008). Grey shaded areas denote NBER recessions.

which eliminates the seasonal component in dividends. For example, we can rewrite $DP_t^{(4)}$ as

$$DP_t^{(4)} = DP_t \left[1 + \frac{1}{DD_t} + \frac{1}{DD_t \, DD_{t-1}} + \frac{1}{DD_t \, DD_{t-1} \, DD_{t-2}} \right], \quad (4.11)$$

and similarly for $d = 12$. The bottom right chart of Figure 7 also shows $DP_t^{(4)}$. We can see how this modified series is purged of this seasonal behavior, which is why it is the preferred choice for empirical work on predicting equity returns.[29]

There is one more important aspect of the dividend-price ratio. As Figure 7 shows, the dividend-price ratio has a strong persistent component, which could indicate evidence of nonstationarity. However, economic theory would suggest that cumulative gross dividend growth and cumulative gross price growth

---

[29] Note that we multiply DP_t by a factor of four so that DP_t and $DP_t^{(4)}$ are on the same scale.

cannot diverge indefinitely. As lucidly described in Cochrane (2007, p.1535), it then must be that the dividend-price ratio forecasts either dividend growth or price growth (or both). This can be seen clearly by inspecting equation (4.6). If the dividend-price ratio is unusually high, then, by equation (4.6), future price growth must, on average, exceed future dividend growth to bring the ratio down. If the dividend-price ratio is unusually low, the opposite must occur. Taken together, this means that equity returns should be predictable by past values of the dividend-price ratio. This is most commonly translated in a predictive regression of the form

$$r_{t+h}^{(h)} = \alpha^{(h)} + \beta^{(h)} \cdot dp_t^{(d)} + \varepsilon_{t+h}^{(h)}, \tag{4.12}$$

where $r_{t+h}^{(h)} = r_{t+1} + \cdots + r_{t+h}$ and

$$r_{t+\ell} := \log(1 + R_{t+\ell}), \qquad dp_t^{(d)} := \log(DP_t^{(d)}). \tag{4.13}$$

The regression described by equation (4.12) has a number of specific peculiarities that make it a challenging setup for accurate inference. First, as we saw in Figure 7, $DP_t^{(d)}$ has a strong persistent component which is inherited by $dp_t^{(d)}$. Second, since high-frequency returns are noisy, empirical researchers work with $r_{t+h}^{(h)}$. The overlapping nature of $r_{t+h}^{(h)}$ also generates a high degree of persistence, raising the specter of spurious correlation between the dependent and explanatory variables. As a result, the finite-sample distribution of the regression t-statistic may differ substantially from one based on conventional asymptotic arguments (e.g., Valkanov, 2003).

Finally, as was the case for bond returns in Sections 2 and 3, the variables on either side of equation (4.12) are jointly generated from the same primitive equity market data (see again, equation (4.4)). This induces a strong negative correlation between contemporaneous equity returns and changes in the (log) dividend-price ratio. The existing literature has endeavored to capture this feature by nesting equation (4.12) in the following generic predictive regression

$$r_{t+h}^{(h)} = \alpha^{(h)} + \beta^{(h)} \cdot x_t + \varepsilon_{t+h}^{(h)} \tag{4.14}$$

$$x_{t+1} = \mu + \rho x_{t-1} + v_{t+1}, \tag{4.15}$$

where $\mathrm{CORR}(\varepsilon_{t+1}^{(1)}, v_{t+1}) \approx -0.98$.[30] We refer throughout the section to this correlation as the degree of endogeneity.

In the next section, we will introduce our bootstrap procedure that accommodates all of the features we have highlighted here, including seasonality, high

---

[30] Over the sample period 1952–2023, we obtain an estimated correlation of −0.979 for quarterly data and −0.989 for monthly data.

persistence, overlapping returns and the definitional relation between returns and the dividend-price ratio.

4.2 A Nonparametric Seasonal Bootstrap

Our resampling procedure exploits the definitions and identities laid out in the previous section. We assume that the empirical researcher observes stock prices and associated dividends for a sample of size $T + 1$. Equation (4.6) implies that if we observed dp_0 along with $(dd_1, \ldots, dd_T)$ and $(pp_1, \ldots, pp_T)$, then we can construct $(dp_1, \ldots, dp_T)$. Furthermore, equation (4.4) can then be used to obtain $(R_1, \ldots, R_T)$.

When annual data are used, there is no seasonality in the data and we can work directly with the standard identities. The corresponding (nonseasonal) block bootstrap algorithm is:

Step 1: Let Z^E be the $T \times 2$ matrix with tth row equal to (pp_t, dd_t). Block bootstrap Z^E using block size M to obtain $(dd_1^*, \ldots, dd_T^*)$ and $(pp_1^*, \ldots, pp_T^*)$.

Step 2: Using the first observation of the sample, dp_0, set $dp_0^* = dp_0$ and obtain $(dp_1^*, \ldots, dp_T^*)$ via

$$dp_t^* = dp_{t-1}^* + dd_t^* - pp_t^*.$$

Step 3: Generate bootstrapped returns as

$$R_{t+1}^* = PP_{t+1}^* + DD_{t+1}^* \cdot DP_t^* - 1,$$

where $PP_t^* = \exp(pp_t^*)$, $DD_t^* = \exp(dd_t^*)$, and $DP_t^* = \exp(dp_t^*)$.

Step 4: Generate h-period cumulative returns as $r_{t+h}^{(h)*} = r_{t+1}^* + \cdots + r_{t+h}^*$, where $r_{t+\ell}^* = \log(1 + R_{t+\ell}^*)$.

Step 5: Repeat Steps 1–4 to obtain B bootstrap samples.

Often, predictive regressions for equity returns rely on other economic or financial variables as predictors. We can straightforwardly modify the bootstrap algorithm to accommodate these variables. Let w_t be a vector of external predictors. For notational simplicity, we assume that we observe w_t for $t = 0, 1, \ldots, T$. We pre-whiten w_t using a VAR(1) as

$$w_{t+1} = \widehat{\mu} + \widehat{\Phi} w_t + \tilde{w}_{t+1}. \qquad (4.16)$$

We can then modify Step 1 and append Z^E with $\tilde{w}_t$ for $t = 1, \ldots, T$ so that we jointly block bootstrap pp_t, dd_t, and $\tilde{w}_t$. We construct the bootstrap counterpart of w_t by re-whitening $\tilde{w}_t^*$ using the estimated coefficients $\widehat{\mu}$ and $\widehat{\Phi}$.[31]

---

[31] Again, as in previous sections, we demean $\tilde{w}_t^*$ before re-whitening.

When monthly or quarterly data are used, we have to modify the resampling procedure to accommodate the pronounced seasonal behavior in the data. For simplicity of presentation, we assume that the observed data begin in either December for monthly data or the fourth quarter for quarterly data so that the $t = 1$ observation represents January or the first quarter, respectively. The corresponding *seasonal* block bootstrap algorithm is:

Step S1: Let Z^E be the $T \times 2$ matrix with tth row equal to (pp_t, dd_t). Block bootstrap a single block from Z^E to obtain $(dd_1^*, \ldots, dd_M^*) = (dd_s, \ldots, dd_{s+M-1})$ and $(pp_1^*, \ldots, pp_M^*) = (pp_s, \ldots, pp_{s+M-1})$, where s is the starting index of the block.

Step S2: Let $\underline{a}$ be the remainder from s divided by d (so that $s = \underline{a} \pmod{d}$). If $\underline{a} > 1$, set $dp_0^* = dp_{(\underline{a}-1)}$. If $\underline{a} = 1$, then set $dp_0^* = dp_0$.

Step S3: Let $\bar{a}$ be the remainder from $s + M - 1$ divided by d (so that $s + M - 1 = \bar{a} \pmod{d}$). Next, choose with equal probability from $(\bar{a} + 1, \bar{a} + 1 + d, \bar{a} + 1 + 2d, \ldots)$ and call this $\bar{a}^\star + 1$. Append $(pp_{a^\star+1}, pp_{a^\star+2}, \ldots, pp_{a^\star+M})$ and $(dd_{a^\star+1}, dd_{a^\star+2}, \ldots, dd_{a^\star+M})$ to the already existing bootstrapped objects.

Step S4: Repeat the previous step until the bootstrap sample size is equal to or exceeds T. Keep the first T observations.

Step S5: Obtain $(dp_1^*, \ldots, dp_T^*)$ via

$$dp_t^* = dp_{t-1}^* + dd_t^* - pp_t^*,$$

using the initial condition, dp_0^*, from Step S2.

Step S6: Generate bootstrapped returns as

$$R_{t+1}^* = PP_{t+1}^* + DD_{t+1}^* \cdot DP_t^* - 1,$$

where $PP_t^* = \exp(pp_t^*)$, $DD_t^* = \exp(dd_t^*)$, and $DP_t^* = \exp(dp_t^*)$.

Step S7: Generate h-period cumulative returns as $r_{t+h}^{(h)*} = r_{t+1}^* + \cdots + r_{t+h}^*$, where $r_{t+\ell}^* = \log(1 + R_{t+\ell}^*)$ along with $DP_t^{(d)*}$ using equation (4.11) for quarterly data or the analogous expression for monthly data.

Step S8: Repeat Steps S1–S7 to obtain B bootstrap samples.

Steps S2 and S3 are designed to accommodate the seasonal nature of monthly and quarterly data. This is best demonstrated by example. Suppose we are working with monthly data and the time index s from Step S1 represents an observation in March ($\underline{a} = 3$). Then, $\underline{a} - 1 = 2$ and so we choose the first February observation of the dividend-price ratio in our sample as the initial condition ($dp_0^* = dp_2$). In order to further build up our block bootstrap, we then consider the time index at the end of our block, $s + M - 1$. Suppose that the time index $s + M - 1$ represents an observation in August.

Then, $\bar{a} = 8$ and so we randomly choose from all September observations in the sample to start the next block of size M. We then repeat this process, each time, respecting the months at the beginning and end of each bootstrap block to ensure that any seasonal behavior is replicated in each bootstrap sample. In the case where there is an external predictor, w_t, we would modify Steps S1 and S3 to jointly block bootstrap using $(\tilde{w}_s, \ldots, \tilde{w}_{s+M-1})$ and $(\tilde{w}_{a^\star+1}, \tilde{w}_{a^\star+2}, \ldots, \tilde{w}_{a^\star+M})$, respectively, with initial condition $w_0^* = w_0$.

Remark 3 *In the bootstrap algorithm, we assume that the dataset begins with either the last month of the year for monthly data or the final quarter of the year for quarterly data. It is straightforward to generalize this to all possible datasets but with more convoluted notation. Instead, we can proceed by example just as in the previous paragraph. In that case, we would still choose the first February observation of the dividend-price ratio in our sample as the initial condition, dp_0^*. The only difference is that the first February observation would no longer be the third observation in the sample. Similarly, we would still randomly choose a September observation from the sample to begin the next block of size M. Thus, the logic of the bootstrap procedure is unchanged in this more general case.* □

Remark 4 *Throughout this section, we focus on bootstrapping a single stock (or portfolio of stocks). However, the algorithm can be straightforwardly modified to accommodate the joint resampling of a collection of stocks or portfolios. For example, suppose we would like to bootstrap N stocks with associated price and dividend growth, $\{(pp_{1,t}, dd_{1,t}), \ldots, (pp_{N,t}, dd_{N,t})\}$. In this case, Z^E is a $T \times 2N$ matrix and we follow the same steps as enumerated except that each bootstrap block of price and dividend growth becomes an $M \times N$ matrix rather than an $M \times 1$ vector. This joint resampling approach can be used for cross-sectional equity applications such as analyzing traded and non-traded factors,[32] assessing trading strategies, and, more generally, quantifying uncertainty in candidate pricing models. Finally, in cases where an individual firm (or collection of firms) does not always pay dividends, we could use a dividend-free set of identities to generate our resampled data (e.g., Vuolteenaho, 2002).* □

In each seasonal nonparametric bootstrap sample, we are appending blocks of the data that preserve the seasonal structure. Thus, in each bootstrap sample we will see, for example, pronounced seasonality in dividends as was the case in Figure 7. Figure 8 shows a single bootstrap draw for returns and the

---

[32] To accommodate non-traded factors, we can simply add these factors to w_t in equation (4.16).

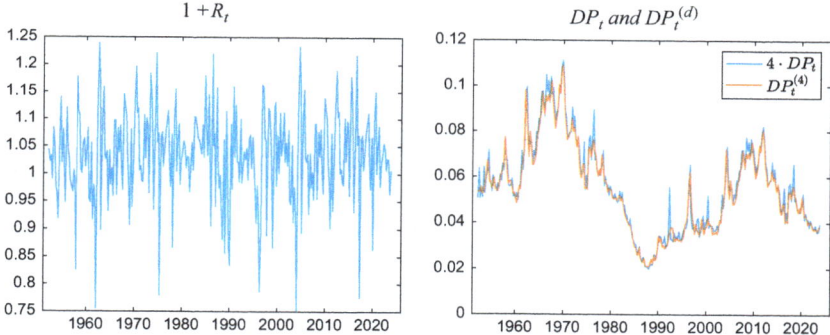

Figure 8 Bootstrapped Sample of Equity Returns. This figure presents the time series and the dividend-price ratio for a single bootstrap draw with $M = 205$. Note that we present the time series of $4 \cdot DP_t$ so it is on the same scale as $DP_t^{(4)}$. The sample period is 1952Q1–2023Q4 using data from Welch and Goyal (2008).

dividend-price ratio based on quarterly data. We omit graphs for PP_t and DD_t since these are the objects we directly block bootstrap and so their properties will be similar to those of their counterparts in Figure 7. The left chart of Figure 8 shows that bootstrapped returns exhibit mild serial correlation as in the data. The right chart shows how our seasonal bootstrap algorithm replicates the key features of the dividend-price ratio. In particular, we can see how the bootstrapped DP_t has additional spikes relative to the smoother $DP_t^{(4)}$.

Our bootstrap is fundamentally different from the existing approaches in the econometrics literature, which utilize a generic predictive regression setup. We retain the flexibility of a nonparametric bootstrap but still generate the correct degree of persistence in both returns and the dividend-price ratio without taking a stand on the true law of motion. To do so, we work with the primitive objects PP_t and DD_t and generate returns and the dividend-price ratio via economic identities. An off-the-shelf bootstrap procedure would not share these properties, which shows the value of tailoring statistical methods to the specific empirical environment.

4.3 Simulation Evidence

In order to evaluate the finite-sample properties of our bootstrap procedure, we need to simulate data with features similar to those of the observed data. Here, we will introduce a simple VAR specification, which ensures that economic identities are respected in the simulated data (e.g., Cochrane, 2007). First, note that taking conditional expectations of equation (4.6) gives

$$\mathbb{E}_{t-1}[dp_t] - dp_{t-1} = \mathbb{E}_{t-1}[dd_t] - \mathbb{E}_{t-1}[pp_t], \quad (4.17)$$

where $\mathbb{E}_{t-1}[\cdot] = \mathbb{E}[\cdot|\mathcal{F}_{t-1}]$ and $\mathcal{F}_t$ is the information set at time t. As noted earlier, in order for dp_t to be stationary, it must be that either pp_t or dd_t (or both) are predictable based on dp_{t-1}. Thus, we assume

$$\mathbb{E}_{t-1}[pp_t] = a_p + b_p dp_{t-1}, \tag{4.18}$$

$$\mathbb{E}_{t-1}[dd_t] = a_d + b_d dp_{t-1}. \tag{4.19}$$

Plugging this into equation (4.17) gives

$$\mathbb{E}_{t-1}[dp_t] = (a_d - a_p) + (1 + b_d - b_p) dp_{t-1}. \tag{4.20}$$

Thus, to ensure stationarity we have the restriction that $b_p > b_d$ (and $b_p - b_d < 2$). More generally, this gives rise to the following system of equations:

$$pp_t = a_p + b_p dp_{t-1} + \eta_t^{pp}, \tag{4.21}$$

$$dd_t = a_d + b_d dp_{t-1} + \eta_t^{dd}, \tag{4.22}$$

$$dp_t = (a_d - a_p) + (1 + b_d - b_p) dp_{t-1} + \left(\eta_t^{dd} - \eta_t^{pp}\right), \tag{4.23}$$

which can be rewritten in a restricted VAR(1) form:

$$g_t = \mu_g + \Phi_g g_{t-1} + \eta_t^g, \tag{4.24}$$

where

$$\mu_g = \begin{bmatrix} a_p \\ a_d \\ a_d - a_p \end{bmatrix} \quad \text{and} \quad \Phi_g = \begin{bmatrix} 0 & 0 & b_p \\ 0 & 0 & b_d \\ 0 & 0 & 1 + b_d - b_p \end{bmatrix}.$$

Although there are three variables in the VAR, there are only two shocks, and we designate the variance-covariance matrix of $(\eta_t^{pp}, \eta_t^{dd})'$ as Σ_η. The law of motion for the data described by equation (4.24) has similarities and key differences relative to the standard approach relying on log-linearizing equation (4.4) (e.g., Campbell & Shiller, 1988a; Cochrane, 2007). Both approaches provide a simple data-generating process, which ensures that economic identities hold and key features of the data are replicated (e.g., the degree of endogeneity found in the data). However, in our approach these identities hold exactly, whereas there remains a linearization error in the conventional approach. On the other hand, the standard approach admits a predictive return equation that is linear in the log dividend-price ratio, whereas the relation is nonlinear when using equation (4.24).

In our simulations, we calibrate the parameters of equation (4.24) from the data. For annual data, we calibrate all parameters over the sample from 1926–2023, whereas for monthly and quarterly data, we use the sample from 1952–2023. Because the actual monthly and quarterly data will have seasonal effects, we rely on $DP_t^{(d)}$ for the calibration. In particular, we estimate an AR(1) for $dp_t^{(d)}$ by OLS to provide an estimate of $a_d - a_p$ and $1 + b_p - b_d$. Importantly, although we rely on $dp_t^{(d)}$ from the data, the model-implied first-order autocorrelations of dp_t and $dp_t^{(d)}$ are almost identical so that we are not calibrating a more persistent process than what is observed in the data. Further, returns and the dividend-price ratio from this process replicate the degree of endogeneity observed in the data.

We then estimate a_p and b_p via a predictive regression of pp_{t+1} on $dp_t^{(d)}$ and infer the value of a_d and b_d based on the other two estimates. To estimate Σ_η, we obtain $\tilde{\eta}_t^0 := (\tilde{\eta}_t^{pp}, \tilde{\eta}_t^{dd})'$ using the calibrated parameters for a_p, a_d, b_p and b_d and construct $\widetilde{\Sigma}_\eta = \widetilde{T}^{-1} \sum_{t=1}^{\widetilde{T}} \tilde{\eta}_t^0 \tilde{\eta}_t^{0\prime}$, where $\widetilde{T} + 1$ is the sample size of the actual data.

To simulate equity data, we use these calibrated parameters and draw the errors, η_t^g, from a joint Gaussian distribution. We choose simulated sample sizes that mimic the data and the empirical application in the next section. For the process calibrated from annual data, we use $T = 100$, from quarterly data we use $T = 300$, and from monthly data we use $T = 400$ and $T = 800$. We focus on inference about $\beta^{(h)}$ in the predictive regression of equation (4.12). As our data-generating process admits a nonlinear relation between future returns and the lagged (log) dividend-price ratio, $\beta^{(h)}$ represents the best-linear predictor coefficient[33]

$$\beta^{(h)} = \frac{\mathbb{C}(r_{t+h}^{(h)}, dp_t^{(d)})}{\mathbb{V}(dp_t^{(d)})}. \tag{4.25}$$

In practice, we obtain $\beta^{(h)}$ via simulation using a very large sample size. We choose values of h suitable for the associated calibration (e.g., one-month, one-year, and two-years-ahead for the monthly calibration). Finally, all results are based on 5,000 simulations. See Section 2.5.3 for full details on calculating empirical size and power across simulations.

For comparison, we also report results for a number of alternative inference approaches. We continue to use the variance estimator from Newey and West (1987) and the equal-weighted cosine (EWC) variance estimator from Lazarus et al. (2018). Since the number of predictors tends to be small in equity return regressions, we also report results based on the lag-augmentation approach of Montiel Olea and Plagborg-Møller (2021) which has been shown to have appealing theoretical properties. In particular, we estimate the regression

---

[33] Although we focus on linear predictive models, nonlinear predictive models have also been considered in the literature (e.g., Adrian, Crump, & Vogt, 2019; Marmer, 2008; Timmermann, 2008). Since our bootstrap is nonparametric, it can also be directly applied to nonlinear regression models such as these.

$$r_{t+h}^{(h)} = \alpha^{(h)} + \beta^{(h)} \cdot dp_t^{(d)} + \beta_-^{(h)} \cdot dp_{t-1}^{(d)} + \epsilon_{t+h}^{(h)}. \qquad (4.26)$$

We form t-statistics for $\beta^{(h)}$ based on an Eicker-White-Huber variance estimator and rely on a standard normal asymptotic approximation.[34] Finally, just as in the previous sections, we report results for the infeasible oracle resampling procedure, which uses the true parameters and law of motion of the data.

To implement the bootstrap procedure from the previous section, we require a choice of block size, M. We design a data-driven rule for use in the simulations of the form

$$\widehat{M} = \widehat{M}_f\left(T, h, \widehat{\rho}_{dp}\right), \qquad (4.27)$$

where f denotes the sampling frequency (e.g., monthly) and $\widehat{\rho}_{dp}$ is the estimated first-order autocorrelation of $dp_t^{(d)}$ in each simulated dataset. We provide full details in Section 4.5.3 of the Appendix.

Table 8 presents the results for our baseline VAR(1) model. The first column of each of the twelve panels shows the empirical size of a t-test centered at the true $\beta^{(h)}$ for each of the inference procedures. We provide results based on a nominal size of 10%. The next column in each panel presents size-adjusted (SA) power for each of the procedures. We start with the annual calibration based on a sample size of $T = 100$. When $h = 1$, the alternative procedures show varying degrees of size distortion. Inference based on HAC/HAR estimators (Newey-West and LLSW) performs the worst, with empirical size approximately double the nominal size. In the bottom two rows, we present the results for our bootstrap and the (infeasible) oracle bootstrap procedure. Our bootstrap is very close to the oracle bootstrap in terms of both size and power across all three forecast horizons.[35]

The next panels in Table 8 present results for the quarterly and monthly calibrations, with sample sizes commonly encountered in applied work. As the sampling frequency increases, the persistence of $dp_t^{(d)}$ also increases, as does the magnitude of the degree of endogeneity. This is reflected in the stark deterioration of the HAC/HAR variance estimators–especially for longer forecast horizons–which can have empirical size higher than 80% versus a nominal size of 10% (see monthly calibration with $T = 400$ and $h = 24$). For $h = 1$, we can look across these three calibrations and see that the lag-augmentation approach provides a good approximation to the sampling behavior of the test statistic.

---

[34] Although Montiel Olea and Plagborg-Møller (2021) show that this approach is asymptotically valid, they recommend a bootstrap-based inference procedure for better performance. For simplicity, and to enable direct comparisons to the other approaches based on asymptotic distributional approximations, we use the plain-vanilla lag-augmentation approach here.

[35] Footnote 11 in Section 2 provides details on interpreting comparisons to the power of the oracle procedure.

Table 8 Equity Return Prediction under a VAR(1). This table presents empirical size and size-adjusted (SA) power for the predictive regression given by equation (4.12). Results are reported for a nominal level of 10%. Each panel corresponds to results using the VAR(1) specification of equation (4.24) calibrated for different sampling frequencies, sample sizes, T, and forecast horizons, h. Based on 5,000 simulations and 399 bootstrap replications per simulation.

	Annual Calibration ($T = 100$)					
	Size	SA Power	Size	SA Power	Size	SA Power
	$h = 1$		$h = 3$		$h = 5$	
Newey-West	0.178	0.462	0.273	0.441	0.315	0.432
LLSW EWC	0.195	0.397	0.220	0.394	0.237	0.377
Lag Aug.	0.133	0.198	0.177	0.291	0.202	0.358
CG	0.109	0.489	0.117	0.451	0.127	0.414
Oracle	0.105	0.467	0.103	0.434	0.100	0.428
	Quarterly Calibration ($T = 300$)					
	$h = 1$		$h = 4$		$h = 8$	
Newey-West	0.270	1.000	0.393	0.999	0.440	0.997
LLSW EWC	0.282	0.988	0.307	0.992	0.343	0.991
Lag Aug.	0.117	0.214	0.176	0.515	0.231	0.698
CG	0.079	0.889	0.076	0.879	0.076	0.869
Oracle	0.100	1.000	0.100	0.998	0.102	0.996
	Monthly Calibration ($T = 400$)					
	$h = 1$		$h = 12$		$h = 24$	
Newey-West	0.760	0.999	0.857	0.977	0.877	0.942
LLSW EWC	0.738	0.961	0.805	0.962	0.857	0.950
Lag Aug.	0.124	0.216	0.454	0.652	0.633	0.805
CG	0.091	0.757	0.084	0.797	0.116	0.783
Oracle	0.103	0.999	0.102	0.975	0.100	0.937
	Monthly Calibration ($T = 800$)					
	$h = 1$		$h = 12$		$h = 24$	
Newey-West	0.683	1.000	0.759	0.999	0.768	0.996
LLSW EWC	0.653	0.998	0.697	0.997	0.739	0.996
Lag Aug.	0.120	0.261	0.326	0.842	0.476	0.935
CG	0.101	0.597	0.066	0.752	0.057	0.862
Oracle	0.105	1.000	0.104	0.999	0.103	0.995

However, the size-adjusted power is much lower than that obtained by our bootstrap procedure. For example, in the quarterly calibration, the size-adjusted power for our bootstrap is 89% as compared to 21% when using the lag-augmented regression. As h grows, the lag-augmentation approach again shows substantial size distortions and can have empirical size as high as 63% versus a nominal size of 10% (see monthly calibration with $T = 400$ and $h = 24$).

In sharp contrast to the alternative procedures, our bootstrap controls size across all three calibrations and forecast horizons. Comparing the size-adjusted power to the (infeasible) oracle bootstrap, we observe that this robustness comes at the expense of some power properties. That said, it is important to remember that the oracle bootstrap uses knowledge of the exact data-generating process. Furthermore, the size-adjusted power of the alternative procedures is of theoretical interest only insofar as they fail to control size in practice. Finally, we emphasize that the data-driven rule for block size engenders meaningful variability across simulations, showing that our procedure is robust to the specific choice of M. For example, for the monthly calibration with $T = 800$ and $h = 1$, $\widehat{M}$ has a 25th percentile of 148 and a 75th percentile of 502. The appropriate block size is much larger for our bootstrap than in conventional applications; however, the results in Table 8 show that this does not undermine the performance of the approach.

Since our bootstrap is nonparametric, we should expect it to continue to perform well across different data-generating processes. As a robustness check we also report results for a VAR(2) specification, which provides more complex dynamics than a VAR(1) specification (see Section 4.5.2 of the Appendix for further details). These results are presented in Table 9. As expected, our method performs very similarly to that in Table 8, with empirical size close to the nominal size of 10% and reasonable power properties. This further demonstrates the advantages of a nonparametric approach. Inference based on HAC/HAR estimators also performs similarly to that in Table 8, with severe size distortions in almost all of the settings we consider. The most substantial difference between Table 8 and Table 9 is the performance of the lag-augmented approach. With a VAR(2) specification adding only one additional lag is insufficient to exploit the advantages of lag augmentation. As such, we observe that the results based on lag augmentation show moderate-to-severe size distortions throughout.

Along with the dividend-price ratio, many papers have argued for a host of additional variables as stock-return predictors (e.g., Goyal, Welch, & Zafirov, 2024). Therefore, we modify our simulation design by adding an additional variable, w_t, which follows an AR(1) process

$$w_t = \mu_w + \phi_w w_{t-1} + \eta_t^w. \tag{4.28}$$

Table 9 Equity Return Prediction under a VAR(2). This table presents empirical size and size-adjusted (SA) power for the predictive regression given by equation (4.12). Results are reported for a nominal level of 10%. Each panel corresponds to results using the VAR(2) specification described in Section 4.5.2 of the Appendix calibrated for different sampling frequencies, sample sizes, T, and forecast horizons, h. Based on 5,000 simulations and 399 bootstrap replications per simulation.

	Size	SA Power	Size	SA Power	Size	SA Power
	\multicolumn{6}{c}{Annual Calibration ($T = 100$)}					
	$h=1$		$h=3$		$h=5$	
Newey-West	0.131	0.494	0.267	0.529	0.329	0.512
LLSW EWC	0.179	0.422	0.229	0.456	0.254	0.446
Lag Aug.	0.238	0.044	0.144	0.217	0.151	0.362
CG	0.113	0.534	0.112	0.570	0.123	0.527
Oracle	0.104	0.486	0.102	0.523	0.104	0.506
	\multicolumn{6}{c}{Quarterly Calibration ($T = 300$)}					
	$h=1$		$h=4$		$h=8$	
Newey-West	0.216	1.000	0.341	0.999	0.397	0.998
LLSW EWC	0.236	0.992	0.269	0.994	0.307	0.995
Lag Aug.	0.301	0.030	0.151	0.346	0.191	0.661
CG	0.061	0.872	0.060	0.873	0.056	0.865
Oracle	0.102	1.000	0.103	0.999	0.103	0.998
	\multicolumn{6}{c}{Monthly Calibration ($T = 400$)}					
	$h=1$		$h=12$		$h=24$	
Newey-West	0.707	0.999	0.819	0.985	0.843	0.958
LLSW EWC	0.689	0.973	0.764	0.975	0.822	0.968
Lag Aug.	0.128	0.096	0.395	0.652	0.599	0.811
CG	0.073	0.793	0.067	0.827	0.094	0.818
Oracle	0.105	0.999	0.099	0.984	0.097	0.959
	\multicolumn{6}{c}{Monthly Calibration ($T = 800$)}					
	$h=1$		$h=12$		$h=24$	
Newey-West	0.631	1.000	0.716	1.000	0.728	0.998
LLSW EWC	0.602	0.999	0.646	0.998	0.700	0.997
Lag Aug.	0.166	0.062	0.278	0.842	0.455	0.938
CG	0.084	0.628	0.052	0.795	0.045	0.904
Oracle	0.102	1.000	0.101	1.000	0.101	0.997

We set $\mu_w = 0$ and choose ϕ_w based on the sampling frequency of the calibration: $\phi_w = 0.9$ for the annual calibration, $\phi_w = 0.95$ for the quarterly calibration, and $\phi_w = 0.98$ for the monthly calibration. We jointly simulate η_t^w so that it has a correlation of 0.3 with η_t^{pp} and unit variance. Importantly, w_t does not predict returns and so we can assess the performance of our bootstrap for distinguishing an extraneous predictor. We jointly bootstrap the equity market variables and the external predictor as discussed in the previous section.

Table 10 presents the results for the VAR(1) data-generating process based on the predictive regression

$$r_{t+h}^{(h)} = \alpha^{(h)} + \beta^{(h)} \cdot dp_t^{(d)} + \gamma^{(h)} \cdot w_t + \varepsilon_{t+h}^{(h)}, \tag{4.29}$$

Table 10 Equity Return Prediction under a VAR(1) with External Predictor. This table presents empirical size for t-statistics associated with $\beta^{(h)}$ and $\gamma^{(h)}$ for the predictive regression given by equation (4.29). Results are reported for a nominal level of 10%. Each panel corresponds to results using the VAR(1) specification of equation (4.24) calibrated for different sampling frequencies, sample sizes, T, and forecast horizons, h. Based on 5,000 simulations and 399 bootstrap replications per simulation.

	Annual Calibration ($T = 100$)					
	$\beta^{(h)}$	$\gamma^{(h)}$	$\beta^{(h)}$	$\gamma^{(h)}$	$\beta^{(h)}$	$\gamma^{(h)}$
	$h=1$		$h=3$		$h=5$	
Newey-West	0.210	0.159	0.306	0.252	0.351	0.283
Hodrick	0.107	0.959	0.098	0.955	0.093	0.947
LLSW EWC	0.221	0.155	0.256	0.187	0.277	0.202
Lag Aug.	0.142	0.118	0.203	0.142	0.230	0.160
CG	0.110	0.069	0.120	0.059	0.129	0.053
Oracle	0.107	0.097	0.108	0.098	0.105	0.100
	Quarterly Calibration ($T = 300$)					
	$\beta^{(h)}$	$\gamma^{(h)}$	$\beta^{(h)}$	$\gamma^{(h)}$	$\beta^{(h)}$	$\gamma^{(h)}$
	$h=1$		$h=4$		$h=8$	
Newey-West	0.307	0.151	0.419	0.231	0.465	0.259
Hodrick	0.177	1.000	0.164	1.000	0.137	1.000
LLSW EWC	0.309	0.157	0.335	0.171	0.366	0.187
Lag Aug.	0.119	0.110	0.191	0.113	0.256	0.134
CG	0.080	0.073	0.077	0.069	0.075	0.070
Oracle	0.097	0.102	0.096	0.098	0.099	0.103

Table 10 (cont.)

	Monthly Calibration ($T = 400$)					
	$\beta^{(h)}$	$\gamma^{(h)}$	$\beta^{(h)}$	$\gamma^{(h)}$	$\beta^{(h)}$	$\gamma^{(h)}$
	$h = 1$		$h = 12$		$h = 24$	
Newey-West	0.749	0.175	0.849	0.298	0.874	0.328
Hodrick	0.637	1.000	0.608	1.000	0.560	1.000
LLSW EWC	0.734	0.184	0.804	0.231	0.856	0.280
Lag Aug.	0.139	0.111	0.485	0.133	0.659	0.158
CG	0.089	0.034	0.082	0.060	0.118	0.096
Oracle	0.105	0.098	0.105	0.102	0.102	0.097
	Monthly Calibration ($T = 800$)					
	$\beta^{(h)}$	$\gamma^{(h)}$	$\beta^{(h)}$	$\gamma^{(h)}$	$\beta^{(h)}$	$\gamma^{(h)}$
	$h = 1$		$h = 12$		$h = 24$	
Newey-West	0.688	0.165	0.767	0.277	0.776	0.287
Hodrick	0.584	1.000	0.546	1.000	0.495	1.000
LLSW EWC	0.667	0.166	0.713	0.203	0.748	0.243
Lag Aug.	0.126	0.108	0.346	0.120	0.496	0.124
CG	0.105	0.041	0.068	0.045	0.060	0.066
Oracle	0.105	0.086	0.102	0.093	0.104	0.097

where $\gamma^{(h)} = 0$. We report empirical size for t-statistics for each predictor based on a nominal size of 10%. Since the data are generated under the null that $\gamma^{(h)} = 0$, we do not report the empirical power for the second coefficient. We omit the empirical power for tests based on the estimated $\beta^{(h)}$ as well, as they exhibit patterns similar to those as in Tables 8 and 9 but are modestly lower. We also additionally compare results to those based on Hodrick (1992) standard errors (referred to as "1B"; see p.362 of Hodrick, 1992). These standard errors enjoy widespread use for equity return predictive inference. Importantly, these standard errors are valid only under the null hypothesis that *no* variables predict future stock returns.

The top panel of Table 10 displays results for the annual calibration. We first observe that for inference on $\beta^{(h)}$, our bootstrap performs very similar to that in Table 8, with empirical size close to nominal size. For the external predictor coefficient, $\gamma^{(h)}$, our bootstrap continues to control size, albeit with some under-rejections especially at longer forecast horizons. However, the modest degree of under-rejections pales in comparison to the over-rejections from all of the feasible methods. For inference on $\beta^{(h)}$, Newey-West, LLSW-EWC and the lag-augmentation approach deteriorate further relative to Table 8.

Regarding the external predictor, only the lag-augmentation approach avoids large size distortions but only for shorter forecast horizons. For example, for the annual calibration with $h = 5$, Newey-West and LLSW-EWC, and the lag-augmentation approach reject the null hypothesis that $\gamma^{(h)} = 0$ in about 28%, 20%, and 16% of the simulations, respectively. Finally, the simulations clearly demonstrate the sensitivity of Hodrick standard errors to the true data-generating process. Since dp_t *does* predict future stock returns in this setting, Hodrick standard errors are no longer valid. Although they control size for inference on $\beta^{(h)}$, they reject the null that $\gamma^{(h)} = 0$ in almost all of the simulations. All of these patterns are similar when we consider the quarterly and monthly calibrations. Our bootstrap continues to control size across these different constellations of the parameters, whereas all other feasible methods fail to control size. One important thing to highlight is that, in the monthly calibration, Hodrick standard errors no longer control size for either coefficient. Finally, Table 11 presents the results for the VAR(2) data-generating process. These results are very similar, with the main exception being that the lag-augmentation approach is misspecified for dp_t and so suffers more meaningful size distortions than in Table 10.

Table 11 Equity Return Prediction under a VAR(2) with External Predictor. This table presents empirical size for t-statistics associated with $\beta^{(h)}$ and $\gamma^{(h)}$ for the predictive regression given by equation (4.29). Results are reported for a nominal level of 10%. Each panel corresponds to results using the VAR(2) specification described in Section 4.5.2 of the Appendix calibrated for different sampling frequencies, sample sizes, T, and forecast horizons, h. Based on 5,000 simulations and 399 bootstrap replications per simulation.

	Annual Calibration ($T = 100$)					
	$\beta^{(h)}$	$\gamma^{(h)}$	$\beta^{(h)}$	$\gamma^{(h)}$	$\beta^{(h)}$	$\gamma^{(h)}$
	$h = 1$		$h = 3$		$h = 5$	
Newey-West	0.169	0.156	0.314	0.250	0.371	0.290
Hodrick	0.079	0.963	0.111	0.983	0.112	0.982
LLSW EWC	0.212	0.148	0.274	0.188	0.295	0.206
Lag Aug.	0.210	0.121	0.153	0.140	0.166	0.165
CG	0.112	0.071	0.117	0.058	0.126	0.052
Oracle	0.108	0.096	0.109	0.099	0.108	0.101

Table 11 (cont.)

	Quarterly Calibration ($T = 300$)					
	$\beta^{(h)}$	$\gamma^{(h)}$	$\beta^{(h)}$	$\gamma^{(h)}$	$\beta^{(h)}$	$\gamma^{(h)}$
	$h = 1$		$h = 4$		$h = 8$	
Newey-West	0.260	0.156	0.379	0.229	0.422	0.259
Hodrick	0.149	1.000	0.159	1.000	0.137	1.000
LLSW EWC	0.276	0.152	0.299	0.169	0.332	0.191
Lag Aug.	0.261	0.109	0.153	0.116	0.202	0.135
CG	0.068	0.070	0.067	0.068	0.060	0.066
Oracle	0.102	0.103	0.096	0.099	0.101	0.102

	Monthly Calibration ($T = 400$)					
	$\beta^{(h)}$	$\gamma^{(h)}$	$\beta^{(h)}$	$\gamma^{(h)}$	$\beta^{(h)}$	$\gamma^{(h)}$
	$h = 1$		$h = 12$		$h = 24$	
Newey-West	0.707	0.173	0.820	0.302	0.844	0.328
Hodrick	0.587	1.000	0.553	1.000	0.494	1.000
LLSW EWC	0.683	0.180	0.766	0.231	0.821	0.281
Lag Aug.	0.125	0.112	0.431	0.131	0.626	0.156
CG	0.075	0.034	0.070	0.062	0.095	0.097
Oracle	0.104	0.099	0.103	0.101	0.099	0.095

	Monthly Calibration ($T = 800$)					
	$\beta^{(h)}$	$\gamma^{(h)}$	$\beta^{(h)}$	$\gamma^{(h)}$	$\beta^{(h)}$	$\gamma^{(h)}$
	$h = 1$		$h = 12$		$h = 24$	
Newey-West	0.640	0.164	0.729	0.272	0.741	0.287
Hodrick	0.527	1.000	0.487	1.000	0.431	1.000
LLSW EWC	0.614	0.164	0.665	0.203	0.708	0.243
Lag Aug.	0.153	0.107	0.298	0.119	0.471	0.122
CG	0.088	0.039	0.056	0.042	0.047	0.068
Oracle	0.103	0.086	0.101	0.091	0.103	0.097

In sum, despite the very challenging inference problem in equity-return predictive regressions, our bootstrap is able to control size across different data-generating processes and parameter values. This is accomplished often with only modest declines in power relative to an infeasible benchmark (the oracle bootstrap). It is important to re-emphasize that our bootstrap is agnostic about the true data-generating process and resamples the data in a way that respects the basic identities linking the primitive objects underpinning stock returns.

4.4 Empirical Application

There is a voluminous empirical literature on stock-return prediction that has been comprehensively summarized in Welch and Goyal (2008) and Goyal, Welch, and Zafirov (2024). We utilize the data from these papers and revisit the predictive ability of the variables considered in Welch and Goyal (2008). We restrict ourselves to this subset for simplicity of presentation and also because these predictors have a longer and uniform sample period. These predictors are the most widely used in the literature and include valuation ratios, information from other asset prices, and macroeconomic variables.

More specifically, we use the earnings-price ratio (e/p), dividend-payout ratio (d/e), stock variance (svar), book-to-market ratio (b/m), net equity expansion (ntis), Treasury-bill rate (tbl), long-term government bond yield (lty), long-term government bond return (ltr), long-term government bond yield less the Treasury-bill rate (tms), default yield spread (dfy), default return spread (dfr), and CPI inflation (infl). We investigate the predictability results for quarterly data for the sample from 1952 to 2023 and monthly data for this sample period and also one starting in 1990.[36] The corresponding sample sizes are 284, 408, and 864, which closely align with our simulation designs in the previous section.

To implement our bootstrap in empirical applications, we recommend using a rule-of-thumb choice that exploits the VAR(1) data-generating process introduced in equation (4.24). Specifically, we calibrate a simulation design to the exact sample period and forecast horizon to find the choice of M (in multiples of five) that minimizes size distortion (nominal level of 10%) for inference on $\beta^{(h)}$ with no external predictors. The specific choices of M are given in Section 4.5.3 of the Appendix. This approach to choosing M is akin to other parametric rules of thumb that are commonly used in the nonparametric literature, such as Silverman's rule of thumb for density estimation. More generally, for users of the bootstrap, we recommend matching the calibration of the VAR(1) to whatever empirical data are being used.

We start by investigating the predictive power of the dividend-price ratio as the sole predictor of future equity returns (i.e., equation (4.12)). The left panel of Table 12 reports the OLS estimate of $\beta^{(h)}$ along with p-values obtained from our bootstrap procedure. This panel also displays p-values obtained using Newey-West standard errors and a standard normal limiting distribution. For all sampling frequencies and forecast horizons considered, our bootstrap

---

[36] Results for annual data and other sample periods can be obtained from the companion MATLAB replication package.

Table 12 Equity Returns and the Dividend-Price Ratio. This table presents regression results for the predictive regression given by equation (4.12). The left panel of the table provides the OLS estimate, $\widehat{\beta}_{OLS}$, along with p-values based on our bootstrap (CG) and the asymptotic approximation using Newey-West standard errors (NW). The right panel is based on a lag-augmentation (LA) approach with one additional lag and presents the corresponding OLS estimate and p-value. Bootstrap p-values are based on the bootstrap procedure introduced in Section 4.2 using B = 1,999.

	Quarterly (1952–2023)				
	$\widehat{\beta}_{OLS}^{(h)}$	CG p-val	NW p-val	$\widehat{\beta}_{LA}^{(h)}$	LA p-val
$h = 1$	0.026	0.00	0.03	−0.045	0.49
$h = 4$	0.029	0.00	0.00	0.025	0.44
$h = 8$	0.026	0.00	0.00	0.047	0.01
	Monthly (1952–2023)				
	$\widehat{\beta}_{OLS}^{(h)}$	CG p-val	NW p-val	$\widehat{\beta}_{LA}^{(h)}$	LA p-val
$h = 1$	0.008	0.01	0.04	−0.012	0.77
$h = 12$	0.009	0.03	0.00	−0.002	0.83
$h = 24$	0.008	0.03	0.00	0.011	0.08
	Monthly (1990–2023)				
	$\widehat{\beta}_{OLS}^{(h)}$	CG p-val	NW p-val	$\widehat{\beta}_{LA}^{(h)}$	LA p-val
$h = 1$	0.020	0.10	0.03	0.035	0.58
$h = 12$	0.020	0.02	0.00	0.004	0.80
$h = 24$	0.021	0.01	0.00	0.011	0.25

procedure rejects the null hypothesis of no predictability at the 10% level or below. Although we obtain similar p-values when using Newey-West standard errors, we saw in the simulations section that this procedure is unlikely to control size in general. The right panel reports results using the lag-augmentation approach with one additional lag. For almost all specifications, the p-value is well above 10%. One possible explanation is that this reflects the lower power of this approach exhibited in the simulations. We should also note that the addition of dp_{t-1} in the regression changes the sign of the estimated $\beta^{(h)}$ from positive to negative in three of the specifications and exhibits sensitivity to the forecast horizon. In contrast, the OLS estimates are more stable across forecast horizons.

Table 13 presents the results for the bivariate predictive regression using the dividend-price ratio and one of the twelve Welch and Goyal (2008) predictors (i.e., equation (4.29)). We start by investigating the p-value for t-statistics associated with $\beta^{(h)}$. For our bootstrap, the results are similar to those in Table 12 with p-values near zero for almost all specifications and forecast horizons. The only exception is when e/p is added as a predictor in which case the evidence is weaker. One possible explanation for this result is the high correlation (0.8 in this sample) between the dividend-price ratio and the earnings-price ratio in these data. In terms of the external predictors, our bootstrap finds only very limited evidence of stock-return predictability at the $h = 24$ horizon. In contrast, both Newey-West and the lag-augmentation approach find substantially more evidence of predictability – especially at longer forecast horizons. This is consistent with the simulation evidence where these two procedures tended to over-reject the null hypothesis.

In Tables 14 and 15 we report results based on monthly data for the sample periods 1952–2023 and 1990–2023, respectively. The results in Table 14 are largely similar to those based on quarterly data. Our bootstrap provides consistent evidence that the dividend-price ratio predicts future returns, whereas there is, at best, only limited evidence in favor of any of the external predictors. As shown in Table 15, when we restrict the sample to start in 1990, the predictive ability of the dividend-price ratio appears somewhat weaker at $h = 1$ but not at longer horizons. This is consistent with the evidence presented in Table 12. Interestingly, all three inference approaches find little evidence of stock-return predictability based on external predictors over this sample period.

The key takeaway of this section is that existing inference procedures used to assess the degree of stock return predictability are likely to have meaningful size distortions. This prompted Welch and Goyal (2008) to focus primarily on out-of-sample forecasting performance rather than in-sample statistical significance. However, as shown in Inoue and Kilian (2005), if in-sample inference is valid, it should be more powerful than out-of-sample performance. We have shown that by coupling in-sample evidence with a trustworthy inference procedure tailored to equity market data, we reach conclusions similar to those based on out-of-sample performance. Overall, we find strong evidence in the data that the dividend-price ratio contains information about future returns as would be suggested by modern asset pricing theory. At the same time, we find little consistent evidence that any of the external predictors considered in Welch and Goyal (2008) have additional information for future equity returns.

Table 13 Equity Returns, the Dividend-Price Ratio, and External Predictors (Quarterly, 1952–2023). This table presents regression results for the predictive regression given by equation (4.29) using external predictors from Welch and Goyal (2008). The top (bottom) portion of each panel reports p-values for the null hypothesis that $\beta^{(h)} = 0$ for dp_t (and $\gamma^{(h)} = 0$ for each predictor w_t). We report p-values based on our bootstrap (CG), the asymptotic approximation using Newey-West standard errors (Newey-West), and a lag-augmentation (Lag Aug.) approach with one additional lag. Bootstrap p-values are based on the bootstrap procedure introduced in Section 4.2 using B = 1,999.

w_t		e/p	d/e	svar	b/m	ntis	tbl	lty	ltr	tms	dfy	dfr	infl
							$h = 1$						
$\beta^{(h)}$	CG	0.12	0.00	0.00	0.01	0.00	0.00	0.00	0.00	0.00	0.00	0.00	0.00
	Newey-West	0.23	0.05	0.03	0.06	0.02	0.00	0.01	0.04	0.02	0.06	0.03	0.01
	Lag Aug.	0.68	0.59	0.35	0.61	0.51	0.68	0.66	0.57	0.54	0.62	0.61	0.76
$\gamma^{(h)}$	CG	0.90	0.42	0.40	0.68	0.57	0.42	0.18	0.55	0.92	0.93	0.99	0.31
	Newey-West	0.94	0.17	0.56	0.33	0.37	0.06	0.18	0.06	0.31	0.57	0.61	0.17
	Lag Aug.	0.87	0.79	0.59	0.21	0.29	0.20	0.07	0.04	0.96	0.51	0.77	0.41
							$h = 4$						
$\beta^{(h)}$	CG	0.08	0.00	0.00	0.02	0.00	0.00	0.00	0.00	0.00	0.00	0.00	0.00
	Newey-West	0.06	0.01	0.00	0.01	0.00	0.00	0.00	0.00	0.00	0.01	0.00	0.00
	Lag Aug.	0.68	0.56	0.89	0.79	0.40	0.21	0.27	0.40	0.33	0.52	0.48	0.12
$\gamma^{(h)}$	CG	0.81	0.30	0.10	0.65	0.60	0.11	0.10	0.71	0.78	0.72	0.88	0.23
	Newey-West	0.79	0.06	0.02	0.18	0.39	0.04	0.24	0.01	0.07	0.35	0.95	0.00
	Lag Aug.	0.80	0.05	0.02	0.58	0.82	0.07	0.01	0.01	0.35	0.22	0.89	0.00

Table 13 (cont.)

w_t		e/p	d/e	svar	b/m	ntis	tbl	lty	ltr	tms	dfy	dfr	infl
							$h=8$						
$\beta^{(h)}$	CG	0.39	0.00	0.00	0.02	0.00	0.01	0.01	0.00	0.00	0.00	0.00	0.00
	Newey-West	0.08	0.00	0.00	0.00	0.00	0.00	0.01	0.00	0.00	0.01	0.00	0.00
	Lag Aug.	0.09	0.02	0.08	0.37	0.01	0.00	0.00	0.01	0.00	0.01	0.02	0.00
$\gamma^{(h)}$	CG	1.00	0.26	0.05	0.57	0.41	0.14	0.49	0.02	0.61	0.26	0.44	0.22
	Newey-West	1.00	0.05	0.00	0.02	0.35	0.08	0.44	0.01	0.01	0.58	0.52	0.00
	Lag Aug.	0.52	0.00	0.02	0.11	0.20	0.09	0.03	0.02	0.12	0.12	0.69	0.01

Table 14 Equity Returns, the Dividend-Price Ratio, and External Predictors (Monthly, 1952–2023). This table presents regression results for the predictive regression given by equation (4.29) using external predictors from Welch and Goyal (2008). The top (bottom) portion of each panel reports p-values for the null hypothesis that $\beta^{(h)} = 0$ for dp_t (and $\gamma^{(h)} = 0$ for each predictor w_t). We report p-values based on our bootstrap (CG), the asymptotic approximation using Newey-West standard errors (Newey-West), and a lag-augmentation (Lag Aug.) approach with one additional lag. Bootstrap p-values are based on the bootstrap procedure introduced in Section 4.2 using B = 1,999.

w_t		e/p	d/e	svar	b/m	ntis	tbl	lty	ltr	tms	dfy	dfr	infl
							$h=1$						
$\beta^{(h)}$	CG	0.18	0.01	0.00	0.21	0.02	0.02	0.01	0.01	0.01	0.01	0.01	0.00
	Newey-West	0.32	0.06	0.05	0.05	0.02	0.00	0.01	0.04	0.03	0.07	0.04	0.01
	Lag Aug.	0.29	0.90	0.88	0.61	0.83	0.92	0.99	0.89	0.83	0.76	0.88	0.89
$\gamma^{(h)}$	CG	0.72	0.59	0.82	0.35	0.29	0.35	0.21	0.98	0.91	0.90	0.57	0.74
	Newey-West	0.85	0.43	0.62	0.28	0.32	0.05	0.16	0.03	0.21	0.54	0.51	0.06
	Lag Aug.	0.25	0.51	0.46	0.30	0.15	0.01	0.03	0.05	0.16	0.58	0.60	0.04
							$h=12$						
$\beta^{(h)}$	CG	0.07	0.02	0.03	0.16	0.03	0.05	0.04	0.03	0.04	0.04	0.03	0.02
	Newey-West	0.05	0.00	0.00	0.00	0.00	0.00	0.00	0.00	0.00	0.01	0.00	0.00
	Lag Aug.	0.51	0.85	0.36	0.88	0.90	0.65	0.77	0.92	0.94	0.86	0.81	0.63
$\gamma^{(h)}$	CG	0.91	0.31	0.11	0.31	0.43	0.11	0.08	0.79	0.77	0.87	0.46	0.27
	Newey-West	0.91	0.07	0.04	0.13	0.40	0.04	0.25	0.00	0.04	0.29	0.79	0.00
	Lag Aug.	0.43	0.02	0.05	0.81	0.94	0.04	0.00	0.00	0.70	0.35	0.95	0.00

Table 14 (cont.)

w_t		e/p	d/e	svar	b/m	ntis	tbl	lty	ltr	tms	dfy	dfr	infl
							$h = 24$						
$\beta^{(h)}$	CG	0.15	0.03	0.03	0.17	0.03	0.05	0.04	0.03	0.05	0.03	0.03	0.03
	Newey-West	0.06	0.00	0.00	0.00	0.00	0.00	0.01	0.00	0.00	0.01	0.00	0.00
	Lag Aug.	0.84	0.06	0.30	0.67	0.06	0.01	0.03	0.04	0.03	0.08	0.08	0.02
$\gamma^{(h)}$	CG	0.85	0.30	0.10	0.23	0.35	0.07	0.43	0.47	0.61	0.56	0.95	0.21
	Newey-West	0.81	0.04	0.01	0.01	0.37	0.07	0.42	0.01	0.02	0.59	0.98	0.00
	Lag Aug.	0.11	0.00	0.02	0.09	0.19	0.04	0.01	0.02	0.19	0.20	0.92	0.00

Table 15 Equity Returns, the Dividend-Price Ratio, and External Predictors (Monthly, 1990–2023). This table presents regression results for the predictive regression given by equation (4.29) using external predictors from Welch and Goyal (2008). The top (bottom) portion of each panel reports p-values for the null hypothesis that $\beta^{(h)} = 0$ for dp_t (and $\gamma^{(h)} = 0$ for each predictor w_t). We report p-values based on our bootstrap (CG), the asymptotic approximation using Newey-West standard errors (Newey-West), and a lag-augmentation (Lag Aug.) approach with one additional lag. Bootstrap p-values are based on the bootstrap procedure introduced in Section 4.2 using B = 1,999.

w_t		e/p	d/e	svar	b/m	ntis	tbl	lty	ltr	tms	dfy	dfr	infl
							$h=1$						
$\beta^{(h)}$	CG	0.18	0.15	0.10	0.26	0.06	0.08	0.18	0.11	0.05	0.03	0.10	0.10
	Newey-West	0.13	0.04	0.02	0.23	0.04	0.03	0.04	0.04	0.00	0.00	0.03	0.03
	Lag Aug.	0.31	0.46	0.43	0.38	0.53	0.57	0.59	0.62	0.47	0.45	0.39	0.57
$\gamma^{(h)}$	CG	0.61	0.61	0.59	0.97	0.82	0.59	0.57	0.75	0.51	0.86	0.71	0.55
	Newey-West	0.23	0.81	0.84	0.98	0.35	0.46	0.42	0.67	0.02	0.27	0.67	0.70
	Lag Aug.	0.00	0.39	0.78	0.50	0.99	0.69	0.77	0.72	0.98	0.57	0.55	0.77
							$h=12$						
$\beta^{(h)}$	CG	0.01	0.04	0.02	0.26	0.12	0.03	0.04	0.02	0.01	0.02	0.02	0.02
	Newey-West	0.00	0.01	0.00	0.08	0.01	0.00	0.00	0.00	0.00	0.00	0.00	0.00
	Lag Aug.	0.22	0.89	0.91	0.80	0.66	0.72	0.82	0.84	0.75	0.61	0.64	0.81
$\gamma^{(h)}$	CG	0.53	0.95	0.42	0.99	0.95	0.94	0.61	0.81	0.39	0.74	0.39	0.15
	Newey-West	0.36	0.96	0.37	0.97	0.35	0.94	0.40	0.71	0.16	0.60	0.49	0.04
	Lag Aug.	0.00	0.28	0.40	0.54	0.08	0.02	0.35	0.59	0.00	0.21	0.73	0.09

Table 15 (cont.)

w_t		e/p	d/e	svar	b/m	ntis	tbl	lty	ltr	tms	dfy	dfr	infl
							$h=24$						
$\beta^{(h)}$													
	CG	0.01	0.02	0.01	0.19	0.09	0.06	0.01	0.01	0.02	0.03	0.01	0.01
	Newey-West	0.00	0.00	0.00	0.00	0.00	0.00	0.00	0.00	0.00	0.00	0.00	0.00
	Lag Aug.	0.93	0.32	0.43	0.88	0.16	0.24	0.25	0.28	0.36	0.20	0.24	0.27
$\gamma^{(h)}$													
	CG	0.50	0.65	0.76	0.52	0.88	0.64	0.58	0.61	0.97	0.66	0.46	0.36
	Newey-West	0.52	0.64	0.76	0.30	0.45	0.49	0.37	0.51	0.97	0.54	0.60	0.07
	Lag Aug.	0.03	0.64	0.47	0.09	0.53	0.05	0.31	0.42	0.02	0.56	0.86	0.25

4.5 Appendix to Section 4

4.5.1 Data Description

This section relies on data from Welch and Goyal (2008) that are available from the authors' website.[37] Full details on the data construction and definition of variables are available in Welch and Goyal (2008) and their online appendix.

4.5.2 Additional Details on Simulation Design

We first describe the VAR(2) process that we use in our simulation experiments. In this case, we assume

$$\mathbb{E}_{t-1}[pp_t] = a_p + b_{p,1} dp_{t-1} + b_{p,2} dp_{t-2} \tag{4.30}$$

$$\mathbb{E}_{t-1}[dd_t] = a_d + b_{d,1} dp_{t-1} + b_{d,2} dp_{t-2}. \tag{4.31}$$

Plugging this into equation (4.17) gives

$$\mathbb{E}_{t-1}[dp_t] = (a_d - a_p)$$
$$+ (1 + b_{d,1} - b_{p,1}) dp_{t-1} + (b_{d,2} - b_{p,2}) dp_{t-2}. \tag{4.32}$$

This can be rewritten in the form of a restricted VAR(2):

$$g_t = \mu_g + \Phi_{g1} \cdot g_{t-1} + \Phi_{g2} \cdot g_{t-2} + \eta_t^g, \tag{4.33}$$

where $\mu_g = (a_p, a_d, a_d - a_p)'$ just as in the VAR(1) case and

$$\Phi_{g1} = \begin{bmatrix} 0 & 0 & b_{p,1} \\ 0 & 0 & b_{d,1} \\ 0 & 0 & 1 + b_{d,1} - b_{p,1} \end{bmatrix}, \quad \Phi_{g2} = \begin{bmatrix} 0 & 0 & b_{p,2} \\ 0 & 0 & b_{d,2} \\ 0 & 0 & b_{d,2} - b_{p,2} \end{bmatrix}.$$

To calibrate the VAR(2), we estimate an AR(2) model by OLS, separately for pp_t and $dp_t^{(d)}$. Let the corresponding parameter estimates for pp_t be $\tilde{a}_p$, $\tilde{b}_{p,1}$, and $\tilde{b}_{p,2}$, and for $dp_t^{(d)}$, be $\tilde{a}_{dp}$, $\tilde{b}_{dp,1}$, and $\tilde{b}_{dp,2}$. Then, we calibrate $\mu_g = (\tilde{a}_p, \tilde{a}_p + \tilde{a}_{dp}, \tilde{a}_{dp})'$. For Φ_{g1}, the last column is calibrated as $(\tilde{b}_{p,1}, \tilde{b}_{p,1} + \tilde{b}_{dp,1} - 1, \tilde{b}_{dp,1})'$ and, for Φ_{g2}, the last column is calibrated as $(\tilde{b}_{p,2}, \tilde{b}_{p,2} + \tilde{b}_{dp,2}, \tilde{b}_{dp,2})'$. Using these calibrated parameters, we then obtain $\tilde{\eta}_t^0 := (\tilde{\eta}_t^{pp}, \tilde{\eta}_t^{dd})'$ and construct $\widetilde{\Sigma}_\eta = \widetilde{T}^{-1} \sum_{t=1}^{\widetilde{T}} \tilde{\eta}_t^0 \tilde{\eta}_t^{0\prime}$, where $\widetilde{T} + 1$ is the sample size of the actual data. To simulate equity data, we use these calibrated parameters and draw the errors, η_t^g, from a joint Gaussian distribution.

4.5.3 Additional Details on the Choice of M

To find a rule for $\widehat{M}$ for the simulations, we perform the following steps. For each sampling frequency, we calibrate the VAR(1) to the data from 1926 to

---
[37] https://sites.google.com/view/agoyal145.

2023 and find the choice of M (in multiples of five) which minimizes size distortion at the 10% nominal level across different choices of h and T. We then fit the following regression:

$$M_j = a_M + b_{M,1}\log(T) + b_{M,2}\log(1-\rho_{dp}) + b_{M,3}\log(h) + \zeta_j, \quad (4.34)$$

where ρ_{dp} is the calibrated first-order autocorrelation coefficient of $dp_t^{(d)}$. We fit this linear equation by OLS and then obtain the rule

$$\widehat{M}(T,\rho_{dp},h) = \exp\left\{\frac{1}{n}\sum_{j=1}^{n}\hat{\zeta}_j^2\right\}$$
$$\times \exp\left\{\hat{a}_M + \hat{b}_{M,1}\log(T) + \hat{b}_{M,2}\log(1-\rho_{dp}) + \hat{b}_{M,3}\log(h)\right\}.$$
$$(4.35)$$

Finally, we restrict $\widehat{M}(T,\rho_{dp},h) \leq 0.9 \cdot T$ to ensure there is sufficient variation across the bootstrap samples.

For the choice of M in our empirical application, we utilize the following choices. For quarterly data over the sample period 1952–2023, we use $M = 205$ for all three forecast horizons, $h \in \{1,4,8\}$. For monthly data over the sample period 1952–2023, we use $M = 675$ for $h = 1$, $M = 665$ for $h = 12$, and $M = 650$ for $h = 24$. For monthly data over the sample period 1990–2023, we use $M = 305$ for $h = 1$, $M = 285$ for $h = 12$, and $M = 275$ for $h = 24$.

5 Epilogue

This monograph has extended the novel resampling approach of Crump and Gospodinov (2025a) developed for the nominal yield curve. In Section 2, we provide additional insights and results for the nominal yield curve beyond what is available in Crump and Gospodinov (2025a). In Section 3, we present a procedure to jointly resample from the nominal and real yield curves simultaneously utilizing the identities linking nominal and real yields and expected inflation. This extension allows for inference on the statistical properties of market-based measures of inflation expectations. We also show that this identity-based approach can be used for infinite-maturity assets such as equities (Section 4). In particular, we introduce a seasonal bootstrap procedure and demonstrate that it mimics the key features of equity market data.

Although this monograph provides an extensive treatment of resampling-based inference in predictive return regressions, there are natural extensions that have not been considered here. First, the applications of these resampling procedures move well beyond inference in predictive returns regressions. They can be used to provide robust inference on parameters estimated in structural asset pricing models. They can be further used to generate sample asset price paths that could be employed for scenario and other policy analyses, risk management or forecasting. As a concrete example, the bootstrap paths could be used to obtain measures of sampling uncertainty for any desired statistic.

Second, the individual results provided in each section can be combined for multi-asset setups. As an example, to resample *excess* equity-market returns we need to jointly resample data from the nominal yield curve and the equity market. This could be achieved by combining the approaches introduced in Sections 2 and 4. Moreover, this has the advantage of accommodating existing empirical results linking stock and bond markets (Cochrane, 2017). We can go further and combine Sections 3 and 4, which would result in bootstrap samples of excess equity returns, breakeven inflation rates, and longer-maturity nominal yields.

A more substantive extension could be tailored to studying the relation between movements in exchange rates and relative interest rate differentials (see, e.g., Engel, 2014). Let $y_{Dt}^{(n)}$ and $y_{Ft}^{(n)}$, for $n = 1, \ldots, N$, be the nominal yield curves for the domestic country (D) and the foreign country (F). Further, define s_t as the log exchange rate between their respective currencies in units of domestic currency per foreign currency. One object of interest is the so-called carry trade. The returns to this trading strategy can be expressed as

$$rc_{t+n}^{(n)} = \Delta s_{t+n} - \left(y_{Dt}^{(n)} - y_{Ft}^{(n)}\right). \tag{5.1}$$

In words, this is the return from a strategy that borrows in the domestic currency and invests these proceeds in the foreign bond market. Under the assumption of uncovered interest parity (UIP), we should have that $\mathbb{E}_t\left[rc_{t+n}^{(n)}\right] = 0$, so the literature has tested UIP using regressions of the form

$$rc_{t+n}^{(n)} = a^{(n)} + b^{(n)} \cdot \left(y_{Dt}^{(n)} - y_{Ft}^{(n)}\right) + \varepsilon_{t+n}^{(n)}. \tag{5.2}$$

The existing literature has predominantly rejected the null hypothesis that $a^{(n)} = 0$ and $b^{(n)} = 1$. This finding has motivated a large literature to study the potential drivers of carry-trade returns, often using predictive regressions of the form,

$$rc_{t+n}^{(n)} = \alpha^{(n)} + \beta^{(n)\prime} x_t + \varepsilon_{t+n}^{(n)}, \tag{5.3}$$

for candidate predictors x_t including $(y_{Dt}^{(n)} - y_{Ft}^{(n)})$.

Equations (5.2) and (5.3) have direct analogies with the study of the expectations hypothesis and the drivers of bond risk premia and so our bootstrap strategy is well-suited to this setting as well (Crump & Gospodinov, 2025a). In this case, just as in Section 2, we can construct Z_D^N and Z_F^N for the domestic and foreign bond markets. If we define $Z^s = (\Delta s_2, \ldots, \Delta s_T)'$, then we can block bootstrap

$$Z = \begin{bmatrix} Z_D^N & Z_F^N & Z^s \end{bmatrix}. \tag{5.4}$$

It seems reasonable to conjecture that this bootstrap should also enjoy the excellent finite-sample properties that have been demonstrated in Crump and Gospodinov (2025a) and the contents of this Element. Revisiting the evidence for UIP and the drivers of carry-trade returns is beyond the scope of this monograph, but we would expect that new insights could be gleaned and some existing results reconsidered. Furthermore, it is straightforward to include additional countries, and the requisite cross exchange rates, to simultaneously bootstrap multiple carry trades and study their joint behavior.

Notation and Abbreviations

OLS	Ordinary least squares
SE($\cdot$)	Standard error
HAC/HAR	Heteroskedasticity and autocorrelation consistent/robust
(V)AR(p)	(Vector) autoregression of order p
i.i.d.	Independent and identically distributed
$A := B$	A is defined as B
$A =: B$	B is defined as A
$\mathbb{E}[\cdot]$	Expectation operator
$\mathbb{E}_t[\cdot]$	Expectation conditional on the information set at time t
$\mathcal{F}_t$	Information set at time t
L_m	$m \times m$ lower triangular matrix of ones
PC/PCA	Principal components/Principal component analysis
$\sin(\cdot), \cos(\cdot)$	Sine function, cosine function
$\mathbb{1}\{A\}$	Indicator function of the event A
R^2	Goodness-of-fit statistic for OLS regression
$\mathbb{C}(\cdot)$	Covariance operator
$\mathbb{V}(\cdot)$	Variance operator
CORR($\cdot$)	Correlation coefficient
e_i	Selection vector for element i
I_m	$m \times m$ identity matrix
$0_m, 0_{m_1 \times m_2}$	$m \times m$ matrix of zeros, $m_1 \times m_2$ matrix of zeros
M	Block size for block bootstrap
B	Number of bootstrap samples

References

Abrahams, M., Adrian, T., Crump, R. K., Moench, E., & Yu, R. (2016). Decomposing real and nominal yield curves. *Journal of Monetary Economics*, *84*, 182–200.

Adrian, T., Crump, R. K., & Vogt, E. (2019). Nonlinearity and flight-to-safety in the risk-return trade-off for stocks and bonds. *Journal of Finance*, *74*(4), 1931–1973.

Andreasen, M. M., Christensen, J. H. E., & Riddell, S. (2021, 10). The TIPS liquidity premium. *Review of Finance*, *25*(6), 1639–1675.

Andrews, D. W. K. (1991). Heteroskedasticity and autocorrelation consistent covariance matrix estimation. *Econometrica*, *59*(3), 817–858.

Ang, A., & Bekaert, G. (2007). Stock return predictability: Is it there? *Review of Financial Studies*, *20*(3), 651–707.

Bauer, M. D., & Hamilton, J. D. (2018). Robust bond risk premia. *Review of Financial Studies*, *31*(2), 399–448.

Campbell, J. Y., & Shiller, R. J. (1988a). The dividend-price ratio and expectations of future dividends and discount factors. *Review of Financial Studies*, *1*(3), 195–228.

Campbell, J. Y., & Shiller, R. J. (1988b). Stock prices, earnings, and expected dividends. *Journal of Finance*, *43*(3), 661–676.

Campbell, J. Y., & Shiller, R. J. (1996). A scorecard for indexed government debt. In B. S. Bernanke & J. J. Rotemberg (Eds.), *NBER Macroeconomics Annual 1996* (Vol. 11, pp. 155–197). MIT Press.

Campbell, J. Y., & Yogo, M. (2006). Efficient tests of stock return predictability. *Journal of Financial Economics*, *81*(1), 27–60.

Cavanagh, C. L., Elliott, G., & Stock, J. H. (1995). Inference in models with nearly integrated regressors. *Econometric Theory*, *11*(5), 1131–1147.

Cieslak, A., & Povala, P. (2015). Expected returns in Treasury bonds. *Review of Financial Studies*, *28*(10), 2859–2901.

Cochrane, J. (2007). The dog that did not bark: A defense of return predictability. *Review of Financial Studies*, *21*(4), 1533–1575.

Cochrane, J. (2017, 03). Macro-finance. *Review of Finance*, *21*(3), 945–985.

Cochrane, J., & Piazzesi, M. (2004). *Reply to Dai, Singleton, and Yang.* (Working paper)

Cochrane, J., & Piazzesi, M. (2005). Bond risk premia. *American Economic Review*, *95*, 138–160.

Cochrane, J., & Piazzesi, M. (2008). *Decomposing the yield curve.* (Working paper)

Cowles, A. (1933). Can stock market forecasters forecast? *Econometrica, 1*(3), 309–324.

Crump, R. K., & Gospodinov, N. (2022a). *Deconstructing the yield curve* (Staff Report No. 884). Federal Reserve Bank of New York.

Crump, R. K., & Gospodinov, N. (2022b). On the factor structure of bond returns. *Econometrica, 90*(1), 295–314.

Crump, R. K., & Gospodinov, N. (2025a). Deconstructing the yield curve. *Review of Financial Studies, 38*(2), 381–421.

Crump, R. K., & Gospodinov, N. (2025b). *How uncertain is the estimated probability of a future recession?* (No. May 29). https://libertystreeteconomics.newyorkfed.org/2025/05/how-uncertain-is-the-estimated-probability-of-a-future-recession/ (Liberty Street Economics Blog)

Crump, R. K., Gospodinov, N., & Volker, D. (2021). *The persistent compression of the breakeven inflation curve* (No. March 22). https://libertystreeteconomics.newyorkfed.org/2021/03/the-persistent-compression-of-the-breakeven-inflation-curve/ (Liberty Street Economics Blog)

Dai, Q., Singleton, K., & Yang, W. (2004). *Predictability of bond risk premia and affine term structure models.* (Working paper)

D'Amico, S., Kim, D. H., & Wei, M. (2018). Tips from TIPS: The informational content of Treasury inflation-protected security prices. *Journal of Financial and Quantitative Analysis, 53*(1), 395–436.

Davison, A. C., & Hinkley, D. V. (1997). *Bootstrap methods and their application.* Cambridge: Cambridge University Press.

Dudley, W. C., Roush, J., & Ezer, M. S. (2009). The case for TIPS: An examination of the costs and benefits. *Economic Policy Review, 15*(1), 1–17.

Efron, B. (1979). Bootstrap methods: Another look at the jackknife. *Annals of Statistics, 7*(1), 1–26.

Engel, C. (2014). Exchange rates and interest parity. In G. Gopinath, E. Helpman, & K. Rogoff (Eds.), *Handbook of international economics* (Vol. 4, pp. 453–522). Elsevier.

Fama, E. F., & French, K. R. (1988). Dividend yields and expected stock returns. *Journal of Financial Economics, 22*(1), 3–25.

Ferson, W. E., Sarkissian, S., & Simin, T. T. (2003). Spurious regressions in financial economics? *Journal of Finance, 58*(4), 1393–1413.

Filipović, D., Pelger, M., & Ye, Y. (2024). *Shrinking the term structure.* (Working Paper, EPFL)

References

Fitzenberger, B. (1998). The moving blocks bootstrap and robust inference for linear least squares and quantile regressions. *Journal of Econometrics, 82*(2), 235–287.

Fleckenstein, M., Longstaff, F. A., & Lustig, H. (2014). The TIPS-Treasury bond puzzle. *Journal of Finance, 69*(5), 2151–2197.

Fleming, M., & Krishnan, N. (2012). The microstructure of the TIPS market. *Economic Policy Review, 18*(1), 27–45.

Giglio, S., & Kelly, B. (2017). Excess volatility: Beyond discount rates. *Quarterly Journal of Economics, 133*(1), 71–127.

Goetzmann, W. N., & Jorion, P. (1993). Testing the predictive power of dividend yields. *Journal of Finance, 48*(2), 663–679.

Gospodinov, N., & Wei, B. (2016). *Forecasts of inflation and interest rates in no-arbitrage affine models* (Working Paper No. 2016–3). Federal Reserve Bank of Atlanta.

Goyal, A., Welch, I., & Zafirov, A. (2024). A comprehensive 2022 look at the empirical performance of equity premium prediction. *Review of Financial Studies, 37*(11), 3490–3557.

Gürkaynak, R. S., Sack, B., & Wright, J. H. (2007). The U.S. Treasury yield curve: 1961 to the present. *Journal of Monetary Economics, 54*(8), 2291–2304.

Gürkaynak, R. S., Sack, B., & Wright, J. H. (2010, January). The TIPS yield curve and inflation compensation. *American Economic Journal: Macroeconomics, 2*(1), 70–92.

Hall, P. (1992). *The bootstrap and Edgeworth expansion.* New York: Springer.

Hansen, B. (2022). *Econometrics.* Princeton, NJ: Princeton University Press.

Hodrick, R. J. (1992). Dividend yields and expected stock returns: Alternative procedures for inference and measurement. *Review of Financial Studies, 5*(3), 357–386.

Horowitz, J. L. (2001). The bootstrap. In J. J. Heckman & E. Leamer (Eds.), *Handbook of Econometrics* (Vol. 5, pp. 3159–3228). Elsevier.

Inoue, A., & Kilian, L. (2005). In-sample or out-of-sample tests of predictability: Which one should we use? *Econometric Reviews, 23*(4), 371–402.

Jansson, M., & Moreira, M. J. (2006). Optimal inference in regression models with nearly integrated regressors. *Econometrica, 74*(3), 681–714.

Kilian, L. (1998). Small-sample confidence intervals for impulse response functions. *Review of Economics and Statistics, 80*(2), 218–230.

Kostakis, A., Magdalinos, T., & Stamatogiannis, M. P. (2014). Robust econometric inference for stock return predictability. *Review of Financial Studies, 28*(5), 1506–1553.

Künsch, H. R. (1989). The jackknife and the bootstrap for general stationary observations. *Annals of Statistics, 17*(3), 1217–1241.

Lahiri, S. N. (2003). *Resampling methods for dependent data.* New York: Springer.

Lazarus, E., Lewis, D. J., Stock, J. H., & Watson, M. W. (2018). HAR inference: Recommendations for practice. *Journal of Business & Economic Statistics, 36*(4), 541–559.

Mankiw, N. G., & Shapiro, M. D. (1985). Trends, random walks, and tests of the permanent income hypothesis. *Journal of Monetary Economics, 16*(2), 165–174.

Mankiw, N. G., & Shapiro, M. D. (1986). Do we reject too often?: Small sample properties of tests of rational expectations models. *Economics Letters, 20*(2), 139–145.

Marmer, V. (2008). Nonlinearity, nonstationarity, and spurious forecasts. *Journal of Econometrics, 142*(1), 1–27.

Montiel Olea, J. L., & Plagborg-Møller, M. (2021). Local projection inference is simpler and more robust than you think. *Econometrica, 89*(4), 1789–1823.

Newey, W. K., & West, K. D. (1987). A simple, positive semi-definite, heteroskedasticity and autocorrelation consistent covariance matrix. *Econometrica, 55*(3), 703–708.

Niebuhr, T., Kreiss, J.- P., & Paparoditis, E. (2017). Some properties of the autoregressive-aided block bootstrap. *Electronic Journal of Statistics, 11*(1), 725–751.

Pflueger, C. E., & Viceira, L. (2016). Return predictability in the Treasury market: Real rates, inflation, and liquidity. In P. Veronesi (Ed.), *Handbook of fixed-income securities* New Jersey: John Wiley and Sons, Inc., 191–209.

Rapach, D., & Zhou, G. (2013). Forecasting stock returns. In G. Elliott & A. Timmermann (Eds.), *Handbook of economic forecasting* (Vol. 2, pp. 328–383). Elsevier.

Rebonato, R. (2015). Return-predicting factors for US Treasuries: On the similarity of "tents" and "bats". *International Journal of Theoretical and Applied Finance, 18*(4), 1–14.

Rebonato, R. (2018). *Bond pricing and yield curve modeling: A structural approach.* Cambridge: Cambridge University Press.

Rebonato, R. (2023). The Q-measure dynamics of forward rates. *Annual Review of Economics, 15*(1), 493–522.

Rebonato, R. (2024). Can the returns of real Treasuries (TIPS) be predicted? *Journal of Fixed Income, 33*(4), 6–17.

Rebonato, R., & El Aouadi, A. (2021). How do the volatilities of rates depend on their level? The "universal relationship" revisited. *Journal of Fixed Income, 30*(4), 17–31.

Rebonato, R., & Nyholm, K. (2025). Why does the Cochrane-Piazzesi model predict Treasury returns? *Journal of Empirical Finance, 84*, 101650.

Rebonato, R., & Zanetti, P. (2023). Does the Cochrane-Piazzesi factor predict? An international resampling perspective. *Journal of Fixed Income, 32*(4), 1–16.

Sack, B., & Elsasser, R. (2004). Treasury inflation-indexed debt: A review of the U.S. experience. *Economic Policy Review, 10*(1), 47–63.

Singh, K. (1981). On the asymptotic accuracy of Efron's bootstrap. *Annals of Statistics, 9*(6), 1187–1195.

Stambaugh, R. F. (1999). Predictive regressions. *Journal of Financial Economics, 54*(3), 375–421.

Timmermann, A. (2008). Elusive return predictability. *International Journal of Forecasting, 24*(1), 1–18.

Valkanov, R. (2003). Long-horizon regressions: Theoretical results and applications. *Journal of Financial Economics, 68*(2), 201–232.

Van Binsbergen, J. H., & Koijen, R. S. J. (2010). Predictive regressions: A present-value approach. *Journal of Finance, 65*(4), 1439–1471.

Vašíček, O. (1977). An equilibrium characterization of the term structure. *Journal of Financial Economics, 5*(2), 177–188.

Vuolteenaho, T. (2002). What drives firm-level stock returns? *Journal of Finance, 57*(1), 233–264.

Wei, M., & Wright, J. H. (2013). Reverse regressions and long-horizon forecasting. *Journal of Applied Econometrics, 28*(3), 353–371.

Welch, I., & Goyal, A. (2008). A comprehensive look at the empirical performance of equity premium prediction. *Review of Financial Studies, 21*, 1455–1508.

Acknowledgments

We dedicate this Element to our families for their unconditional love and support.

We also thank Riccardo Rebonato, the editor of this Element, for encouraging us to undertake this project and providing feedback and support throughout the process.

Finally, we thank our collaborators, Desi Volker and Peter Van Tassel, who helped develop some of the material in Sections 3 and 4, respectively. Oliver Kim and Charles Smith provided excellent research assistance.

The views expressed in this monograph are our own and do not necessarily reflect those of the Federal Reserve Bank of Atlanta, the Federal Reserve Bank of New York or the Federal Reserve System.

Cambridge Elements

Quantitative Finance

Riccardo Rebonato
EDHEC Business School

Editor Riccardo Rebonato is Professor of Finance at EDHEC Business School and holds the PIMCO Research Chair for the EDHEC Risk Institute. He has previously held academic positions at Imperial College, London, and Oxford University and has been Global Head of Fixed Income and FX Analytics at PIMCO, and Head of Research, Risk Management and Derivatives Trading at several major international banks. He has previously been on the Board of Directors for ISDA and GARP, and he is currently on the Board of the Nine Dot Prize. He is the author of several books and articles in finance and risk management, including *Bond Pricing and Yield Curve Modelling* (2017, Cambridge University Press).

About the Series

Cambridge *Elements in Quantitative Finance* aims for broad coverage of all major topics within the field. Written at a level appropriate for advanced undergraduate or graduate students and practitioners, *Elements* combines reports on original research covering an author's personal area of expertise, tutorials and masterclasses on emerging methodologies, and reviews of the most important literature.

Cambridge Elements

Quantitative Finance

Elements in the Series

Machine Learning for Asset Managers
Marcos M. López de Prado

Advances in Retirement Investing
Lionel Martellini and Vincent Milhau

A Practitioner's Guide to Discrete-Time Yield Curve Modelling: With Empirical Illustrations and MATLAB Examples
Ken Nyholm

Girsanov, Numeraires, and All That
Patrick S. Hagan and Andrew Lesniewski

Causal Factor Investing: Can Factor Investing Become Scientific?
Marcos M. López de Prado

The Behavioral Economics and Politics of Global Warming: Unsettling Behaviors
Hersh Shefrin

Hydrodynamics of Markets: Hidden Links Between Physics and Finance
Alexander Lipton

Deep Learning in Quantitative Trading
Zihao Zhang and Stefan Zohren

Resampling Asset Prices: An Identity-Based Approach
Richard K. Crump and Nikolay Gospodinov

A full series listing is available at: www.cambridge.org/EQF

For EU product safety concerns, contact us at Calle de José Abascal, 56–1°, 28003 Madrid, Spain or eugpsr@cambridge.org.

www.ingramcontent.com/pod-product-compliance
Lightning Source LLC
LaVergne TN
LVHW021950060526
838200LV00043B/1962